SIMPLY

THE BEST

BARBECUE

RECIPES

WENDY HOBSON

EDITED BY CAROLYN HUMPHRIES

foulsham

LONDON • NEW YORK • TORONTO • SYDNEY

foulsham

The Publishing House, Bennetts Close,
Cippenham, Slough, Berkshire, SL1 5AP, England

ISBN 0-572-02417-7

Copyright © 1998 W. Foulsham & Co. Ltd.
Originally published under the title *Quick & Easy Barbecue Inspirations*

Illustrations and cover artwork by Sophie Azimont

Printed in Great Britain by Cox & Wyman Ltd., Reading, Berks

SIMPLY
THE BEST
BARBECUE
RECIPES

CONTENTS

INTRODUCTION

Unless you happen to live in a place where long, hot summers are the norm, a barbecue is most likely to be an impromptu occasion – and that's certainly so in the UK. Of course, we sometimes plan a barbecue party or invite friends round a week or more in advance, but how many stories have you heard about the cook spending the party barbecuing under the carport or in the garage while everyone else sheltered inside from the torrential rain?

On the other hand, a lovely, sunny weekend can easily take us by surprise, and what better way to take advantage of the weather than to have a barbecue – whether it is just for the family, or for neighbours and friends. And while the good old faithfuls – chops, steaks, spare ribs, sausages or burgers – are fun if you don't serve them too often, even a moderate summer with quite a few barbecuing opportunities can mean that they begin to lose their appeal.

So what can you do if you decide to have a barbecue at the last minute? You want ideas that are simple and quick to prepare; don't involve vast lists of unusual and expensive ingredients, overnight marinades or *cordon bleu* sauces; and show you ways of making old favourites such as chicken breasts, burgers or sausages interesting and imaginative. And here they are! You'll find ideas on extras to keep in the cupboard or freezer during the barbecue season, new ways with those old favourites, simple and speedy marinades and interesting and inspiring recipes for you to enjoy throughout the barbecue season. And if the worst comes to worst, they all taste great cooked under the conventional grill (broiler) too!

Notes on the Recipes

* When following a recipe, use either metric, imperial or American measures, do not mix different sets of measurements.

* All spoon measurements are level: 1 tsp = 5 ml;
                                                                1 tbsp = 15 ml.

* Eggs are medium unless otherwise stated.

* Use your favourite good-quality light oil, like sunflower or groundnut (peanut) oil, unless otherwise stated.

* All preparation and cooking times are approximate.

* Always wash and peel, if necessary, all fresh produce before use.

* Where fresh herbs are used, they are specified in the ingredients. You can substitute dried herbs as long as they have time to cook; never use them for sprinkling on finished dishes. If you use dried rather than fresh herbs, use no more than half the stated quantity as they are very pungent. Packets of frozen chopped herbs such as parsley and mint are much better than the dried varieties.

* Always pre-heat the barbecue for about 30 minutes before cooking (see page 13).

* Soak wooden skewers for about 1 hour before cooking to prevent charring.

BARBECUE BASICS

Here are some simple guidelines on getting the best
out of your barbecue, and being ready for that quick
and easy, inspirational meal!
Barbecuing is a straightforward technique which gives
great results, but it is not an exact science. You cannot
really control the temperature of the charcoal; so you
must control the distance you place the food from the
heat – the nearer the food is to the heat, the higher the
temperature and the faster the food will cook. Being over
a direct heat, of course, the food cooks first on the outside,
so you must allow it enough time to cook right through.
This means that larger pieces of food, such as whole fish
or steaks, need to be placed further from the coals,
otherwise they will be charred on the outside before they
are cooked inside. These principles apply whether you
have a tiny Hibachi or a large gas-fired barbecue, and you
will have to experiment and get to know your own
equipment in order to get the best out of it.

Equipment

You can manage with your ordinary kitchen tools, of course but, if you are an enthusiast, it is a good idea to have a few long-handled utensils to make it easier when you are cooking on the barbecue. Only buy what you need; fancy gadgets are more often than not a waste of space. Your barbecue itself can be as small and simple or as impressive as you want – it doesn't make that much difference to the taste of the food!

Most people find briquettes of compressed charcoal are the easiest to use. They burn more slowly and at a higher temperature than lump charcoal, although this can light more quickly so is useful for starting the barbecue. If you really get hooked on the barbecue habit, you'll start to consider a bigger and better barbecue, perhaps with an electric or battery-operated spit and motor.

For the Fire

* Charcoal, firelighters, tapers, matches.
* Foil to line the barbecue (it makes it easier to clear up).
* Tongs for spreading the coals.
* Poker for flicking grey ash off the charcoal.
* Sprinkler bottle of water to douse flare-ups.
* Small shovel for adding coals and clearing ash.
* Bellows for encouraging the fire if it is dying down; blowing is hot and dirty work.
* Pile of sand for dousing the fire after cooking.
* Bucket of water just in case.
* Cleaning materials; specialist ones are available from barbecue suppliers which you may find are more effective than ordinary kitchen cleansers.

For the Food

* Tongs and spatula with long wooden handles for turning foods.
* Basting brush with long wooden handle and a jug.
* Kebab skewers; always soak wooden skewers in cold water for at least 1 hour before use so that they do not char when cooking.
* Hinged wire grilles to hold soft food between layers of mesh so that it doesn't break up during cooking. They are ideal for fish, burgers or other similar foods.
* Knives, forks, chopping board.
* Foil for covering and wrapping food.
* Heat-resistant gloves and large apron.
* Trolley or small table for holding foods etc.

For the Guests

* Serving table.
* Crockery and cutlery, including serving cutlery.
* Drinks and glasses. Bottle and can openers, water jug, ice bucket.
* Tablecloth and sturdy napkins.
* Condiments and relishes.

Safety

* Set up the barbecue on a stable, level surface in the open air, avoiding any overhanging trees or nearby low bushes.
* Light the fire carefully and make sure it is always attended.
* Never move a lighted barbecue.
* Never touch any part of the barbecue once it has been lit. Extremely hot charcoal will look white and powdery rather than glowing red.
* Avoid plastic- or metal-handled tools as they can melt or hold the heat.
* Douse flare-ups quickly.
* Dispose of ashes carefully when they are thoroughly cold.
* Immerse burns immediately in cold water and keep the burn under water until it feels cool. Cover with a dry, sterile dressing, if necessary, and seek medical attention if severe.

Lighting and Maintaining the Fire

* Tell your neighbours you are about to light a barbecue – especially if they have washing out!
* Line the barbecue with foil, shiny side up. Open the vents if the barbecue has them.
* Arrange a few pieces of broken firelighters on the bed.
* Top with a few pieces of lump charcoal or wood chips.
* Arrange a few charcoal briquettes on top.
* Light the firelighters with a taper.

✳ When the charcoal has caught and is burning steadily, use long-handled tongs to spread the charcoal in a single layer and add more charcoal at the edges.

✳ Gradually add charcoal around the outside of the fire to keep it at a steady temperature; putting charcoal on top will smother it. Remember that the charcoal will maintain heat for some time, so don't add more coals if you are coming to the end of cooking.

✳ Douse the fire with sand when you have finished cooking and leave to cool completely.

Starting to Cook

✳ The fire should take about 30 minutes to reach cooking temperature, by which time the charcoal will be grey and powdery.

✳ Oil the rack lightly, then set it about 10 cm/4 in above the coals.

✳ The fire is ready if you can hold your hand just above the rack for only 2–3 seconds.

✳ The centre of the charcoal will always be hotter than the edges, so you can use this to good effect when arranging your food on the rack. Allow plenty of space around the foods so that you can turn them easily and they are not too crowded to cook evenly.

✳ Plan your cooking order in advance so that you start with the foods with the longest cooking times.

✳ Remember that you can arrange your dessert foods on the barbecue and watch them cook while you are enjoying your main course.

Freezer and Store-cupboard Stand-bys

If you like barbecuing, it makes sense to keep a few things handy in the cupboard or the freezer during the barbecue season so that you can create some interesting dishes at short notice. Start with some basics, and you'll soon learn the ingredients and seasonings you use most often.

In the Cupboard

* Spices such as cayenne, cinnamon, coriander (cilantro), cumin, nutmeg, ginger.
* Dried or freeze-dried herbs such as bay leaves, oregano, rosemary, tarragon, thyme.
* Sauces such as soy sauce, Tabasco sauce, tomato purée (paste), Worcestershire sauce, relishes and pickles.
* Seasonings such as salt and pepper (of course!), capers, mustard, pesto sauce, sesame seeds.
* Vinegars such as white and red wine vinegar, balsamic vinegar or fruit vinegars.
* Lemon juice or other citrus juices.
* Olive or groundnut (peanut) oil, sesame oil.
* Garlic, onions and fresh root ginger.
* Honey, sugar, golden (light corn) syrup, treacle (molasses).
* Canned vegetables, pulses or vegetable mixtures such as lentils, tomatoes, ratatouille.
* Canned fruits such as passion fruit, peaches, lychees.
* Canned meats or fish such as anchovies, salmon, tuna.
* Crackers or melba toast.

In the Freezer

* Large prawns (shrimps) or shellfish such as scallops – both great for kebabs.

* Firm-fleshed fish such as monkfish – buy it when you see it on special offer, prepare it in chunks and freeze ready to use for seafood skewers.

* Whole fish such as trout – simple to barbecue and delicious with a butter sauce.

* Good quality beefburgers, a selection of different sausages, cocktail sausages and bacon.

* Good quality meats suitable for grilling (broiling), such as steak, chicken breasts and minced (ground) meat such as beef, lamb or pork.

* Lamb or pork chops.

* Part-baked baguettes or interesting continental breads.

* Ready-to-use herbs such as parsley.

Basic Cooking Times

If you prefer to cook just your favourite simple foods and perhaps add a few interesting sauces or vegetables, here are some cooking times for quick reference. They are based on cooking food from room temperature on a well-heated barbecue. Remember that times are approximate and will vary depending on the thickness of the food, the temperature of the fire, and the distance you place the food from the fire.

Avoid testing food repeatedly by piercing it with a fork or skewer as this will dry it out.

If you are spit-roasting a chicken or a large joint, allow about 30 minutes per 450 g/1 lb. Beef or lamb can be served while it is still slightly pink in the middle. Pork or chicken must be thoroughly cooked through so that the juices run clear when pierced through the thickest part of the meat.

Food	Size	Cooking time on each side
Beefburger	2.5 cm/1 in thick	6 minutes
Beef steak	2.5 cm/1 in thick	5–8 minutes
Chicken breast		10 minutes
Chicken portion		20–30 minutes
Duck breast		10–15 minutes
Fish	large whole	10–12 minutes
	small whole	3–5 minutes
Fish steaks	2.5 cm/1 in thick	3–5 minutes
Ham steaks	1 cm/½ in thick	5 minutes
Lamb chop or steak	2.5 cm/1 in thick	8 minutes
Meat kebab	whole skewer	10–12 minutes
Pork chop or steak	2.5 cm/1 in thick	13 minutes
Sausages	standard	8 minutes
Seafood kebab	whole skewer	5–8 minutes

MARINADES, RUBS AND SAUCES

If you have made a last-minute decision to have a barbecue, and especially if you don't have unusual meats or fish to cook, a marinade can help you create a whole range of different flavours.

If time is short, an overnight marinade is not much use, so all these marinade recipes need only a couple of hours to work their magic, although you can marinate for longer if you have the time, especially with stronger-flavoured meats such as beef. Lighter foods, such as seafoods, will absorb marinade flavours quickly, so often just a short marinating time is all that is necessary to create unusual dishes.

Marinades will also help to tenderise meats, especially cheaper cuts, making it possible to use the chuck steak you have in the fridge, for example, with success. As soon as you have decided on your menu, your main course can be steeping away in flavourful herbs and spices while you get everything else ready.

There's lots of choice here, so that you can use different marinades on the simplest of basic ingredients, using whatever you have to hand.

Wine Marinade

Use this marinade for white meat and firm vegetables such as cauliflower florets, onions, chicory (Belgian endive) or (bell) peppers. Substitute red wine for white and add a finely chopped garlic clove for red meat and game and marinate for at least 2 hours.

Makes about 450 ml/³/₄ pt/ 2 cups

	METRIC	IMPERIAL	AMERICAN
Onion, chopped	1	1	1
Sprigs of parsley	2	2	2
Sprig of tarragon or thyme	1	1	1
Bay leaf	1	1	1
Dry white wine	300 ml	½ pt	1¼ cups
White wine vinegar or lemon juice	30 ml	2 tbsp	2 tbsp
Clear honey	10 ml	2 tsp	2 tsp
Oil	30 ml	2 tbsp	2 tbsp
Juniper berries, crushed	5 ml	1 tsp	1 tsp
Salt and freshly ground black pepper			

1 Whisk together all the ingredients.

2 Marinate foods for at least 30 minutes, preferably longer.

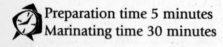
Preparation time 5 minutes
Marinating time 30 minutes

Oriental Marinade

This lighter marinade is ideal for vegetables such as carrots and mangetout (snow peas), seafood or chicken. Substitute 30 ml/ 2 tsp of lemon juice if you do not have lime juice. Do not use a metal container.

Makes about 450 ml/³⁄₄ pt/2 cups

	METRIC	IMPERIAL	AMERICAN
Lime juice	45 ml	3 tbsp	3 tbsp
Rice wine or white wine vinegar	45 ml	3 tbsp	3 tbsp
Light soy sauce	30 ml	2 tbsp	2 tbsp
Dry sherry	15 ml	1 tbsp	1 tbsp
Sesame oil	15 ml	1 tbsp	1 tbsp
Groundnut (peanut) oil	60 ml	4 tbsp	4 tbsp
Light brown sugar	15 ml	1 tbsp	1 tbsp
Chinese five-spice powder	2.5 ml	¹⁄₂ tsp	¹⁄₂ tsp
Large sprig of coriander (cilantro), chopped			

1 Mix together the lime juice, vinegar, soy sauce, sherry and sesame oil. Gradually whisk in the oil.

2 Stir in the remaining ingredients.

3 Marinate foods for at least 2 hours.

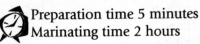
Preparation time 5 minutes
Marinating time 2 hours

Thai-style Marinade

Try this with prawns (shrimp), chicken, seafood kebabs, beef or pork. Foods will benefit from a slightly longer marinating time but this is not essential. You can buy Thai fish sauce, called nam pla, and lemon grass in most large supermarkets. Never use metal bowls for marinades which contain citrus juices. Substitute 45 ml/3 tbsp of lemon juice if you do not have lime juice.

Makes about 450 ml/³/₄ pt/2 cups

	METRIC	IMPERIAL	AMERICAN
Lime juice	75 ml	5 tbsp	5 tbsp
Thai fish sauce	45 ml	3 tbsp	3 tbsp
Sesame oil	175 ml	6 fl oz	³/₄ cup
Garlic cloves, crushed	2–3	2–3	2–3
Roasted peanuts, crushed	45 ml	3 tbsp	3 tbsp
Light brown sugar	25 ml	1¹/₂ tbsp	1¹/₂ tbsp
Lemon grass stalk, chopped	1	1	1
Dried chilli, crushed	2.5 ml	¹/₂ tsp	¹/₂ tsp
Chopped fresh coriander (cilantro)	45 ml	3 tbsp	3 tbsp

1 Mix together the lime juice and fish sauce. Gradually whisk in the sesame oil.

2 Add the remaining ingredients.

3 Marinate foods for at least 2 hours.

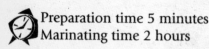

Preparation time 5 minutes
Marinating time 2 hours

Yoghurt Marinade

Ideal for any seafoods, especially salmon or trout, you can make this marinade with any of your favourite herbs.

Makes about 450 ml/³/₄ pt/2 cups

	METRIC	IMPERIAL	AMERICAN
Plain yoghurt	300 ml	½ pt	1¼ cups
Chopped fresh dill (dillweed)	60 ml	4 tbsp	4 tbsp
Grated horseradish	30 ml	2 tbsp	2 tbsp
Grain mustard	30 ml	2 tbsp	2 tbsp
Red wine vinegar	30 ml	2 tbsp	2 tbsp
Olive oil	45 ml	3 tbsp	3 tbsp

1 Mix together all the ingredients except the oil, then gradually whisk in the oil.

2 Marinate foods for at least 1 hour.

Preparation time 5 minutes
Marinating time 1 hour

Sesame Lemon Marinade

This gives a tangy flavour to any seafood or chicken. Use a glass or ceramic bowl.

Makes about 450 ml / ¾ pt / 2 cups

	METRIC	IMPERIAL	AMERICAN
Lemon juice	90 ml	6 tbsp	6 tbsp
Grated lemon rind	15 ml	1 tbsp	1 tbsp
Groundnut (peanut) oil	200 ml	7 fl oz	scant 1 cup
Sesame seeds	45 ml	3 tbsp	3 tbsp
Garlic cloves, crushed	2–3	2–3	2–3
Ground cumin	5 ml	1 tsp	1 tsp
Dried oregano	5 ml	1 tsp	1 tsp
Chopped fresh parsley	60 ml	4 tbsp	4 tbsp
Salt and freshly ground black pepper			

1 Mix together the lemon juice and rind. Gradually whisk in the oil.

2 Toast the sesame seeds in a dry pan until golden, then crush lightly.

3 Add all the remaining ingredients to the lemon juice and oil, seasoning generously with salt and pepper.

4 Marinate foods for at least 1 hour.

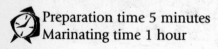
Preparation time 5 minutes
Marinating time 1 hour

Garlic Marinade

Garlic is always a favourite barbecue flavour and this is ideal for any meats.

Makes about 450 ml/¾ pt/2 cups

	METRIC	IMPERIAL	AMERICAN
Dry white wine	300 ml	½ pt	1¼ cups
Olive oil	120 ml	4 fl oz	½ cup
Bay leaf	1	1	1
Garlic cloves, crushed	2	2	2
Sugar	2.5 ml	½ tsp	½ tsp
Salt and freshly ground black pepper			

1 Whisk together all the ingredients.

2 Marinate foods for at least 30 minutes.

3 Use any remaining marinade to baste foods while cooking.

Preparation time 5 minutes
Marinating time 30 minutes

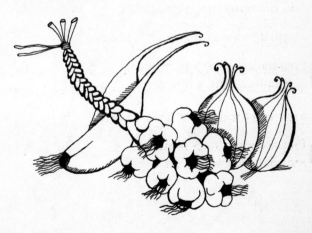

Mediterranean Marinade

A rich Italian-style marinade for seafood or chicken.

Makes about 450 ml / ¾ pt / 2 cups

	METRIC	IMPERIAL	AMERICAN
Lemon juice	75 ml	5 tbsp	5 tbsp
Balsamic vinegar	90 ml	6 tbsp	6 tbsp
Olive oil	200 ml	7 fl oz	scant 1 cup
Garlic cloves, crushed	3	3	3
Canned anchovies, mashed	2	2	2
Capers, drained and chopped	5 ml	1 tsp	1 tsp
Small onion, chopped	1	1	1
Chopped fresh parsley	45 ml	3 tbsp	3 tbsp
Salt and freshly ground black pepper			

1 Mix together the lemon juice and vinegar, then gradually whisk in the oil.

2 Add the remaining ingredients.

3 Marinate foods for at least 2 hours.

Preparation time 5 minutes
Marinating time 2 hours

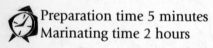

Caribbean Marinade

Try using a sliced ripe mango or pawpaw instead of the passion fruit. If you don't have lime juice, use 45 ml/3 tbsp of lemon juice instead. Use the marinade for seafood, chicken or pork spare ribs. Use a glass or ceramic bowl.

Makes about 450 ml/¾ pt/2 cups

	METRIC	IMPERIAL	AMERICAN
Passion fruit	6	6	6
Orange juice	120 ml	4 fl oz	½ cup
Garlic cloves, crushed	3	3	3
Dark rum	30 ml	2 tbsp	2 tbsp
Black treacle (molasses)	30 ml	2 tbsp	2 tbsp
Lime juice	60 ml	4 tbsp	4 tbsp
Tabasco sauce	5 ml	1 tsp	1 tsp
Ground coriander (cilantro)	2.5 ml	½ tsp	½ tsp
Ground cumin	2.5 ml	½ tsp	½ tsp
Chopped fresh coriander	30 ml	2 tbsp	2 tbsp

1 Scrape out the flesh and seeds of the passion fruit into a small pan with the orange juice and simmer for 5 minutes. Rub through a sieve (strainer) and discard the seeds.

2 Mix with the remaining ingredients.

3 Marinate foods for at least 2 hours.

4 Use any remaining marinade as a sauce.

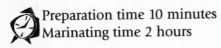
Preparation time 10 minutes
Marinating time 2 hours

Cranberry Marinade

Raspberries or strawberries will also work for this recipe, which tastes great served with chicken or other poultry.

Makes about 450 ml/¾ pt/2 cups

	METRIC	IMPERIAL	AMERICAN
Fresh or frozen cranberries	225 g	8 oz	2 cups
White wine or fruit vinegar	60 ml	4 tbsp	4 tbsp
Small onion, chopped	1	1	1
Garlic clove, crushed	1	1	1
Clear honey	15 ml	1 tbsp	1 tbsp
Lemon juice	45 ml	3 tbsp	3 tbsp
Groundnut (peanut) oil	60 ml	4 tbsp	4 tbsp
Chopped fresh tarragon or parsley	15 ml	1 tbsp	1 tbsp
Salt and freshly ground black pepper			

1 Cook the cranberries in a little water until the skins burst.

2 Leave to cool slightly, then rub through a sieve (strainer).

3 Mix thoroughly with the remaining ingredients.

4 Marinate foods for at least 2 hours, preferably longer.

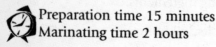

Preparation time 15 minutes
Marinating time 2 hours

Ginger Sweet and Sour Marinade

Chicken, pork or kebabs all benefit from the oriental flavours of this marinade. If you use it for beef, it will need to steep for several hours. Do not use a metal bowl.

Makes about 450 ml/³/₄ pt/2 cups

	METRIC	IMPERIAL	AMERICAN
Hoisin sauce	30 ml	2 tbsp	2 tbsp
Soy sauce	60 ml	4 tbsp	4 tbsp
Clear honey	15 ml	1 tbsp	1 tbsp
Lime juice	120 ml	4 fl oz	½ cup
Sesame oil	30 ml	2 tbsp	2 tbsp
Groundnut (peanut) oil	75 ml	5 tbsp	5 tbsp
Garlic cloves, crushed	2	2	2
Small onion, finely chopped	1	1	1
Chopped fresh coriander (cilantro)	45 ml	3 tbsp	3 tbsp
Grated fresh root ginger	15 ml	1 tbsp	1 tbsp
Star of anise	1	1	1
Piece of cinnamon stick	2.5 cm	1 in	1 in

1 Mix together the hoisin and soy sauces, honey and lime juice. Gradually add the oils.

2 Stir in the remaining ingredients.

3 Marinate foods for at least 3 hours.

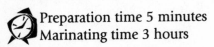
Preparation time 5 minutes
Marinating time 3 hours

Rich Plum Sauce Marinade

A rich marinade that gives a wonderful glaze to barbecued foods – try it with chicken, duck or spare ribs. You can leave it overnight if you have time. You can buy the plum sauce in supermarkets, or substitute a sweet relish.

Makes about 450 ml/¾ pt/2 cups

	METRIC	IMPERIAL	AMERICAN
Dry sherry	30 ml	2 tbsp	2 tbsp
Oriental plum sauce	150 ml	¼ pt	⅔ cup
Soy sauce	15 ml	1 tbsp	1 tbsp
Hoisin sauce	15 ml	1 tbsp	1 tbsp
Sesame oil	5 ml	1 tsp	1 tsp
Groundnut (peanut) oil	30 ml	2 tbsp	2 tbsp
Grated fresh root ginger	15 ml	1 tbsp	1 tbsp
Garlic cloves, crushed	2	2	2
Chopped fresh coriander (cilantro)	60 ml	4 tbsp	4 tbsp

1   Mix together the sherry, the plum, soy and hoisin sauces and the sesame oil. Gradually whisk in the groundnut oil.

2   Mix in the remaining ingredients.

3   Marinate foods for at least 3 hours.

Preparation time 5 minutes
Marinating time 3 hours

Rosemary Rub

If you make rubs with all dry ingredients, you can make a larger quantity and keep them in the freezer, ready for use; try making this one with garlic powder. This is lovely with chicken or lamb. Oil your barbecue rack well before cooking.

Makes about 120 ml/ 4 fl oz/ ½ cup

	METRIC	IMPERIAL	AMERICAN
Chopped fresh rosemary	60 ml	4 tbsp	4 tbsp
Garlic cloves, crushed	2	2	2
Mustard powder	5 ml	1 tsp	1 tsp
Dried oregano	5 ml	1 tsp	1 tsp
Pinch of cayenne			
Salt and freshly ground black pepper			

1 Blend or grind all the ingredients to a coarse powder.

2 Rub all over the meat and leave to stand for at least 2 hours.

Preparation time 5 minutes
Marinating time 2 hours

Cajun Rub

Try this on pork spare ribs, chicken or beef. Oil the barbecue rack well before cooking.

Makes about 150 ml / ¼ pt / ⅔ cup

	METRIC	IMPERIAL	AMERICAN
Garlic cloves, crushed	2	2	2
Finely chopped onion	30 ml	2 tbsp	2 tbsp
Paprika	45 ml	3 tbsp	3 tbsp
Cayenne	15 ml	1 tbsp	1 tbsp
Dried sage	5 ml	1 tsp	1 tsp
Dried thyme	5 ml	1 tsp	1 tsp
Dried oregano	10 ml	2 tsp	2 tsp
Light brown sugar	15 ml	1 tbsp	1 tbsp
Salt and freshly ground black pepper			

1 Blend or grind all the ingredients, seasoning generously with salt and pepper. Add extra cayenne if you like a really hot flavour.

2 Rub over meats and leave to stand for at least 3 hours.

 Preparation time 5 minutes
Marinating time 3 hours

Quick Barbecue Sauce

Serve this easy sauce with any meat, fish or vegetables from the barbecue.

Serves 4

	METRIC	IMPERIAL	AMERICAN
Butter or margarine	50 g	2 oz	¼ cup
Onion, chopped	1	1	1
Tomato purée (paste)	5 ml	1 tsp	1 tsp
Red wine vinegar	30 ml	2 tbsp	2 tbsp
Light brown sugar	30 ml	2 tbsp	2 tbsp
Mustard powder	10 ml	2 tsp	2 tsp
Worcestershire sauce	30 ml	2 tbsp	2 tbsp
Water	150 ml	¼ pt	⅔ cup

1 Melt the butter or margarine and fry (sauté) the onion until soft.

2 Add the remaining ingredients, stirring together over a low heat until well blended.

3 Bring to the boil, then simmer for 10 minutes.

4 Serve warm or cold.

Preparation time 10 minutes
Cooking time 10 minutes

Spicy Orange and Tomato Sauce

Serve this with chicken, vegetables or strongly flavoured fish such as mackerel.

Makes about 450 ml/³/₄ pt/2 cups

	METRIC	IMPERIAL	AMERICAN
Butter or margarine	100 g	4 oz	¹/₂ cup
Tomato purée (paste)	250 ml	8 fl oz	1 cup
White wine vinegar	250 ml	8 fl oz	1 cup
Horseradish sauce	45 ml	3 tbsp	3 tbsp
Light brown sugar	45 ml	3 tbsp	3 tbsp
Grated rind and juice of 1 large orange			
Lemon juice	30 ml	2 tbsp	2 tbsp
Worcestershire sauce	15 ml	1 tbsp	1 tbsp
Salt			

1 Simmer all the ingredients for about 30 minutes, stirring occasionally, until thick.

2 Serve warm or cold.

Preparation time 5 minutes
Cooking time 30 minutes

Quick Chinese Sauce

This sauce will keep in the fridge for several weeks in an airtight jar.

Makes about 450 ml/³/₄ pt/2 cups

	METRIC	IMPERIAL	AMERICAN
Hoisin sauce	250 ml	8 fl oz	1 cup
Rice wine or white wine vinegar	120 ml	4 fl oz	½ cup
Garlic cloves, crushed	2–3	2–3	2–3
Soy sauce	60 ml	4 tbsp	4 tbsp
Chopped fresh root ginger	15 ml	1 tbsp	1 tbsp
Chinese five-spice powder	5 ml	1 tsp	1 tsp

1 Simmer all the ingredients over a low heat for 10 minutes.

2 Serve hot or warm.

 Preparation time 5 minutes
Cooking time 10 minutes

Mustard Sauce

The stronger the mustard you use, the stronger the flavour of the sauce. Reheat sauces by standing them in a flameproof container next to the barbecue coals. This sauce is particularly good with beef, sausages or oily fish.

Makes about 450 ml/³/₄ pt/2 cups

	METRIC	IMPERIAL	AMERICAN
White wine vinegar	250 ml	8 fl oz	1 cup
Made mustard	175 ml	6 fl oz	³/₄ cup
Onion, finely chopped	¹/₂	¹/₂	¹/₂
Garlic cloves, crushed	4	4	4
Water	75 ml	5 tbsp	5 tbsp
Tomato purée (paste)	60 ml	4 tbsp	4 tbsp
Paprika	15 ml	1 tbsp	1 tbsp
Cayenne	2.5 ml	¹/₂ tsp	¹/₂ tsp
Salt and freshly ground black pepper			

1 Gently simmer all the ingredients for about 20 minutes, stirring occasionally, until the onion is soft and the sauce thick.

2 Serve warm or cold.

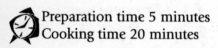
Preparation time 5 minutes
Cooking time 20 minutes

Indonesian Hot Peanut Sauce

Serve this with chicken, beef or pork kebabs.

Serves 4

	METRIC	IMPERIAL	AMERICAN
Water	120 ml	4 fl oz	½ cup
White wine vinegar	120 ml	4 fl oz	½ cup
Sugar	50 g	2 oz	½ cup
Peanut butter	100 g	4 oz	½ cup
Grated fresh root ginger	30 ml	2 tbsp	2 tbsp
Garlic clove, crushed	1	1	1
Soy sauce	45 ml	3 tbsp	3 tbsp
Chopped fresh coriander (cilantro)	15 ml	1 tbsp	1 tbsp
Pinch of cayenne			
Salt			
Sesame oil	15 ml	1 tbsp	1 tbsp

1 Boil the water, vinegar and sugar for 5 minutes, stirring to dissolve the sugar. Remove from the heat and leave to cool.

2 Purée the mixture with all the remaining ingredients except the oil until smooth.

3 Blend in the oil.

4 Serve warm.

Preparation time 5 minutes
Cooking time 5 minutes

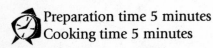

Treacly Apple Sauce

Serves 4

	METRIC	IMPERIAL	AMERICAN
Butter or margarine	50 g	2 oz	¼ cup
Onion, finely chopped	1	1	1
Eating (dessert) apple, peeled and finely chopped	1	1	1
Apple juice	450 ml	¾ pt	2 cups
Black treacle (molasses)	30 ml	2 tbsp	2 tbsp
Worcestershire sauce	15 ml	1 tbsp	1 tbsp
Cider vinegar	15 ml	1 tbsp	1 tbsp
Ground cinnamon	5 ml	1 tsp	1 tsp

1   Melt the butter or margarine and fry (sauté) the onion until soft.

2   Stir in the remaining ingredients until well blended. Bring to a boil, then simmer for about 25 minutes until thickened, stirring regularly.

3   Serve warm.

 Preparation time 10 minutes
Cooking time 25 minutes

Last-minute Sauce Ideas

* Remember fruit sauces complement barbecued meats: apple sauce, cranberry sauce, redcurrant jelly (clear conserve). You don't have to make your own as there are many good brands available.

* Blend plain yoghurt or soured (dairy sour) cream with some snipped fresh chives, salt and pepper. Good with jacket potatoes and all spicy foods.

* Use ramekin dishes (custard cups) arranged on a platter to serve a selection of ready-made sauces and relishes: tomato ketchup (catsup), horseradish sauce, tartare sauce, brown sauce, mint sauce, cucumber relish, sweet pickle – whatever you have available that fits the food.

* Heat passata (sieved tomatoes) with a little dried basil and season to taste.

* Mix equal quantities of tomato ketchup (catsup), golden (light corn) syrup, and vinegar with soy and Worcestershire sauce to taste. Use for basting or as a serving sauce.

* Use a vacuum jug or flask to keep sauces hot; many are attractive enough to be used as serving jugs.

Flavoured Butters

Blend any of these flavour combinations into 100 g/
4 oz/½ cup of softened unsalted butter, then roll and chill
before slicing on to barbecued meats or vegetables.

* 1 crushed garlic clove, 15 ml/1 tbsp chopped fresh
  herbs (such as parsley, basil, rosemary, tarragon or
  oregano), salt and freshly ground black pepper.

* 15 ml/1 tbsp toasted sesame seeds (see page 64), 5 ml/
  1 tsp sesame oil, 1 finely chopped spring onion
  (scallion), salt and freshly ground black pepper.

* 15 ml/1 tbsp chopped fresh mint, 15 ml/1 tbsp made
  mustard, salt and finely ground black pepper.

* 5 ml/1 tsp chilli powder, a few drops of Tabasco sauce,
  salt and freshly ground black pepper.

* 75 g/3 oz/¾ cup crushed almonds, plenty of salt and a
  little freshly ground black pepper.

* 3 crushed anchovy fillets, 1 crushed garlic clove and
  freshly ground black pepper.

* 3 drained, chopped sun-dried tomatoes in oil, 15 ml/
  1 tbsp chopped fresh basil and freshly ground black
  pepper.

* 50 g/2 oz/⅓ cup finely chopped stoned (pitted) olives,
  10 ml/2 tsp finely chopped capers, 15 ml/1 tbsp
  chopped fresh parsley and freshly ground black pepper.

* 100 g/4 oz/1 cup crumbled blue cheese, a pinch of
  paprika and 30 ml/2 tbsp plain yoghurt.

WHY ARE WE WAITING?

As the wonderful aroma of barbecuing food begins to drift across the garden, you'll find that everyone begins to get very hungry. A little thought in advance will keep them busy with nibbles, simple starters, dips and finger foods to stave off those hunger pangs until the main course is ready. It will make you feel much more relaxed about the barbecue foods if you know your guests are not desperate to eat!

~~~~~~~~~~~~~~~~~

Marinated Mozzarella and Olives

This is really best if left overnight, and can be kept in a jar in the fridge for a week. Serve it with crusty bread or a fresh tomato salad.

Serves 4

	METRIC	IMPERIAL	AMERICAN
Mozzarella cheese, cut into chunks	450 g	1 lb	4 cups
Stoned (pitted) black olives	75 g	3 oz	½ cup
Dry white wine	120 ml	4 fl oz	½ cup
Olive oil	120 ml	4 fl oz	½ cup
Lemon juice	30 ml	2 tbsp	2 tbsp
Sun-dried tomatoes in oil, drained and chopped	50 g	2 oz	⅓ cup
Garlic cloves, crushed	2–3	2–3	2–3
Chopped fresh parsley	30 ml	2 tbsp	2 tbsp
Chopped fresh basil	30 ml	2 tbsp	2 tbsp
Pinch of cayenne			
Salt and freshly ground black pepper			

1 Place the cheese and olives in a large wide-mouthed jar or bowl with a lid.

2 Blend together the remaining ingredients and pour over the cheese and olives. Marinate in the fridge for at least 3 hours, preferably longer.

Preparation time 10 minutes
Marinating time 3 hours

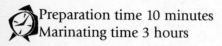

Smoked Salmon with Horseradish Butter on Rye

Smoked salmon pieces are much cheaper than slices, and you can buy them frozen or vacuum packed for convenience.

Serves 4

	METRIC	IMPERIAL	AMERICAN
Rye bread slices	4	4	4
Butter or margarine, softened	40 g	1½ oz	3 tbsp
Horseradish sauce	30 ml	2 tbsp	2 tbsp
A few drops of lemon juice			
Salt and freshly ground black pepper			
Smoked salmon, cut into slivers	100 g	4 oz	¼ lb
Chopped fresh parsley	15 ml	1 tbsp	1 tbsp

1 Cut the bread into about 2.5 cm/1 in squares.

2 Blend or beat together the butter or margarine, horseradish, lemon juice, salt and pepper. Spread on the bread squares.

3 Arrange the salmon on top and garnish with parsley.

 Preparation time 15 minutes

Cantonese Mushroom Kebabs

Serves 4

	METRIC	IMPERIAL	AMERICAN
Button mushrooms	225 g	8 oz	½ lb
Can of water chestnuts, drained	230 g	8 oz	1 small
Soy sauce	90 ml	6 tbsp	6 tbsp
Dry sherry	30 ml	2 tbsp	2 tbsp
Groundnut (peanut) oil	30 ml	2 tbsp	2 tbsp
Light brown sugar	15 ml	1 tbsp	1 tbsp
Garlic clove, crushed	1	1	1
Grated fresh root ginger	5 ml	1 tsp	1 tsp
To serve:			
Bean sprouts	175 g	6 oz	1½ cups

1   Thread the mushrooms and water chestnuts alternately on soaked wooden skewers. Lay them in a shallow dish.

2   Mix the remaining ingredients together and pour over. Turn to coat completely.

3   Marinate in the fridge for at least 3 hours, preferably overnight.

4   Barbecue for 3–4 minutes until the mushrooms are just tender. Serve the kebabs on a small pile of bean sprouts.

Preparation time 10 minutes
Marinating time 3 hours (or overnight)
Cooking time 3–4 minutes

Chilled Cucumber Soup with Dill

Serves 4

	METRIC	IMPERIAL	AMERICAN
Cucumber	1	1	1
Salt and freshly ground black pepper			
Chopped fresh dill (dill weed)	30 ml	2 tbsp	2 tbsp
Cider vinegar	30 ml	2 tbsp	2 tbsp
Plain yoghurt	300 ml	½ pt	1¼ cups
Cold milk	300 ml	½ pt	1¼ cups

1 Cut four slices off the cucumber and reserve for garnish. Grate the remainder into a bowl.

2 Sprinkle with salt and leave to stand for 10 minutes. Squeeze out all the moisture and pour away.

3 Add a good grinding of pepper, the dill, vinegar and yoghurt. Chill until ready to serve.

4 Just before serving, stir in the cold milk, ladle into bowls and float a slice of cucumber on each to garnish.

 Preparation time 15 minutes plus chilling

Spanish Almond Soup

Gazpacho is a well-known Spanish chilled soup – here is another more unusual chilled soup from Spain.

Serves 4

	METRIC	IMPERIAL	AMERICAN
Ground almonds	100 g	4 oz	1 cup
Garlic cloves, crushed	2	2	2
Water	900 ml	1½ pts	3¾ cups
Fresh breadcrumbs	75 g	3 oz	1½ cups
Olive oil	75 ml	5 tbsp	5 tbsp
Sherry vinegar	15 ml	1 tbsp	1 tbsp
Salt and freshly ground black pepper			

1 Purée the almonds and garlic with a little of the water to make a paste.

2 Mix in the breadcrumbs, then gradually beat in the oil. Add the vinegar and enough of the remaining water to make the consistency you prefer. Season with salt and pepper.

3 Chill well before serving.

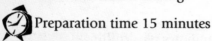 Preparation time 15 minutes

Or if you do want to serve gazpacho: purée 450 g/1 lb ripe tomatoes (or a can), ½ peeled cucumber, 1 red or green (bell) pepper, 1 onion, 15 ml/1 tbsp sherry vinegar, 120 ml/ 4 fl oz/½ cup olive oil and 100 g/4 oz/2 cups fresh breadcrumbs until smooth. Chill well and serve with ice cubes.

Easy Finger Foods

Concentrate on bite-sized nibbles so you don't have to bother with cutlery. Serve crisps, nuts and other interesting nibbles.

* Roll slices of salami on to a cocktail stick (toothpick) with a cube of cucumber or melon or a clementine segment.

* Fill celery sticks with any flavoured soft cheese and cut into short lengths.

* Slice the top off cherry tomatoes and scoop out the insides. Fill with garlic-and-herb-flavoured soft cheese, softened slightly with a little plain yoghurt or milk.

* Push a stuffed olive into stoned (pitted) ready-to-eat prunes or dried apricots.

* Roll thin slices of any interesting cold meats – smoked ham, salami, garlic sausage and so on – round a spoonful of cream cheese flavoured with fresh herbs and pine nuts.

* Wrap chunks of melon, kiwi fruit or figs in slices of prosciutto.

* Spread unsalted butter or Mascarpone cheese on slices of ciabatta and top with sliced black olives and an anchovy fillet or two.

* Top thick slices of cucumber with a spoonful of garlic-flavoured mayonnaise (see page 134) and top with a few cooked, peeled prawns (shrimp) and a sprig of dill (dill weed).

* Drain canned tuna or salmon and season well with wine vinegar, a little salt and plenty of freshly ground black pepper. Thinly slice and butter a baguette and cut the slices in half. Top with the fish and a slice of cucumber or sprig of fresh parsley.

* Put drained, smoked mussels or oysters on small squares of buttered toast and sprinkle with snipped fresh chives.

* Spread slices of toast with low-fat soft cheese. Cut in small triangles and top with Danish lumpfish roe.

Quick and Easy Dips

The easiest choice has to be to buy a selection of dips from the supermarket – and why not? There's a great range and they taste good. If you want to cheat a bit, transfer them to ramekin dishes (custard cups) and arrange on a serving platter. Otherwise, just take off the lids!

Experiment with dips based on whatever you have to hand, or brighten up bought dips with a few extra spices or chopped ingredients. Always taste as you go along and adjust the ingredients to personal taste.

Purée the following dips for a smooth texture, or chop the ingredients finely.

* **Tuna dip:** 250 ml/8 fl oz/1 cup fromage frais, 185 g/ 6½ oz/1 small can drained and flaked tuna, salt and freshly ground black pepper.

* **Guacamole:** 2 peeled and mashed avocados, 1 crushed garlic clove, 30 ml/2 tbsp lemon juice, 15 ml/1 tbsp olive oil, 2.5 ml/½ tsp ground coriander (cilantro), a few drops of Tabasco sauce, salt and freshly ground black pepper.

* **Minted soured cream dip:** 250 ml/8 fl oz/1 cup soured (dairy sour) cream, 30 ml/2 tbsp chopped fresh mint, salt and freshly ground black pepper.

* **Tomato dip:** 200 g/7 oz/1 small can drained and chopped tomatoes, 45 ml/3 tbsp tomato purée (paste), 15 ml/1 tbsp chopped fresh basil, a few drops of Worcestershire sauce, salt and freshly ground black pepper.
* **Blue cheese dip:** 225 g/8 oz/2 cups crumbled or grated blue cheese, 1 small finely chopped onion, 15 ml/ 1 tbsp white wine vinegar, 75 ml/5 tbsp soured (dairy sour) cream (or cream, plain yoghurt or fromage frais and 5 ml/1 tsp lemon juice), salt and freshly ground black pepper.
* **Smoked mackerel dip:** 225 g/8 oz/½ lb skinned and flaked smoked mackerel fillets, 100 g/4 oz/½ cup cottage cheese, 120 ml/4 fl oz/½ cup fromage frais, 50 g/2 oz/¼ cup melted butter or margarine, 15 ml/ 1 tbsp lemon juice, a pinch of cayenne, salt and freshly ground black pepper.
* **Avocado dip:** purée the flesh of an avocado with 1 garlic clove, 225 g/8oz/1 cup cream cheese, 15 ml/ 1 tbsp lemon juice and 15 ml/1 tbsp snipped fresh chives.
* Flavour mayonnaise (see page 134), or fromage frais, or cream cheese, or thick plain yoghurt (or a combination) to taste with one of the following: crushed anchovies; grain mustard; chopped fresh herbs; crushed garlic; chopped gherkins (cornichons); tomato chutney and a few drops of Worcestershire sauce; cayenne or chilli powder; curry powder or paste.

Delicious Dunkers

* A bowl of raw vegetables cut into thin julienne strips makes a colourful table centre and the perfect accompaniment to a selection of dips. Go for all the old favourites if you like them: carrot, cucumber, celery, various coloured (bell) peppers. But also try cauliflower florets, baby carrots, sugarsnap peas, mangetout (snow peas), chicory (Belgian endive), different mushrooms or pieces of blanched asparagus.

* Fruits also offer an interesting counterpoint. Try pieces of star fruit, pear, apple, melon, pineapple, peach or apricot.

* Tortilla chips, corn chips and strips of pitta bread are also great for dipping.

* Don't forget grissini, melba toast or crackers.

* Finger-shaped croûtons of bread fried (sautéed) until golden with a crushed clove of garlic have a wonderful flavour and texture.

* Cut the peelings from well-scrubbed potatoes in short lengths. Put on a baking sheet sprinkled with salt. Bake at 200°C/ 400°F/gas mark 6 for 20 minutes until crisp.

Crispy Potato Skins

Now very popular, these are so easy to make. You can serve them as a vegetable dish or as a starter with dips. Quantities don't really matter – just be warned to make twice as much as you think you'll need as they are very moreish. Use the potato flesh for other recipes. Add chopped fresh herbs or a little cayenne for added flavour.

Serves 4

	METRIC	IMPERIAL	AMERICAN
Potatoes	4	4	4
Olive oil			
Coarsely ground salt			
Freshly ground black pepper			

1 Bake the potatoes in a preheated oven at 200°C/ 400°F/gas mark 6 for about 1 hour or until soft to the touch. Alternatively, pierce the skins with a fork and microwave until tender; four potatoes will take about 12 minutes on high. Leave to cool slightly.

2 Cut the potatoes into quarters and scoop out most of the insides, leaving the skins and a thin layer of potato flesh.

3 Arrange the potato skins in a shallow flameproof dish, brush them generously with olive oil, then sprinkle with lots of salt and a little pepper.

4 Return to the hot oven for about 20 minutes, or grill (broil) until browned and crisp, turning and brushing again once or twice.

Preparation and cooking time 1½ hours

Fake Foccaccia

Use as much onion as you can pile on the pitta breads and as much garlic as you dare.

Serves 4

	METRIC	IMPERIAL	AMERICAN
Olive oil	45 ml	3 tbsp	3 tbsp
Onions, sliced	6	6	6
Garlic cloves, chopped	3	3	3
Pitta breads	4	4	4
Salt and freshly ground black pepper			

1   Heat the oil and fry (sauté) the onions and garlic until soft but not browned.

2   Brush the pitta breads on one side with a little more oil. Pile the onion and garlic mixture on top and season generously with salt and pepper.

3   Cook under a hot grill (broiler) for about 5 minutes until browned on top.

Preparation time 10 minutes
Cooking time 15 minutes

Savoury Cheese Twists

Makes about 60

	METRIC	IMPERIAL	AMERICAN
Frozen puff pastry, thawed	250 g	9 oz	1 packet
Yeast extract	15 ml	1 tbsp	1 tbsp
Cheddar cheese, finely grated	50 g	2 oz	½ cup
To glaze:			
Beaten egg			

1 Roll out the pastry on a lightly floured surface to a 30 cm/12 in square.

2 Spread the yeast extract over, then sprinkle with the cheese.

3 Fold the square in half and roll over again lightly with the rolling pin to seal in the filling.

4 Brush lightly with beaten egg, then cut into thin strips.

5 Hold each end of a strip and twist, then place on a dampened baking sheet. Repeat with each strip.

6 Bake in a preheated oven at 220°C/425°F/gas mark 7 for about 10 minutes until crisp and golden. Serve warm or cold.

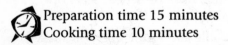
Preparation time 15 minutes
Cooking time 10 minutes

Easy Hot Ideas

* Roll half-rashers (slices) of streaky bacon round mushrooms or stoned (pitted) prunes and grill (broil) until crisp.

* Thread large prawns (shrimp) on to soaked wooden skewers, brush with oil and barbecue for a few minutes. Serve with garlic mayonnaise (see page 134).

* Barbecue or grill (broil) kebabs made with cubes of salami and pineapple.

* Spread slices of bread with mustard and sprinkle with slivers of ham. Top with grated cheese and grill (broil) until sizzling. Cut into fingers and serve.

* Wrap cubes of cheese in squares of filo pastry and brush with oil, then chill until required. Bake in a very hot preheated oven at 220°C/425°F/gas mark 7 for a few minutes until golden.

* Bite-sized sausage rolls may seem uninspired, but they are a good filler or back-up starter and are so easy straight from the freezer. Serve with a flavoured mayonnaise (see page 134) to dip them in.

* Dip button mushrooms in flour, then in egg and fine breadcrumbs. Deep-fry quickly in hot oil until crisp. Serve with a dip (see pages 46–7) if liked.

* Brush cocktail frankfurters with a mixture of redcurrant jelly (clear conserve), soy sauce and tomato chutney. Barbecue on foil, turning, until browned. Serve on cocktail sticks (toothpicks).

* Thread cubes of pineapple and Camembert on soaked wooden skewers. Barbecue briefly on foil, turning occasionally, until the cheese is just melting. Serve straight away.

SEAFOOD

Seafood of all kinds is delicious cooked on the barbecue. Use firm-fleshed fish for kebabs so that it does not fall apart. Wrap fish fillets in foil with a tasty marinade or sauce. Or flash-grill prawns (shrimp) or delicate shellfish to give them that wonderful smoky flavour. Most seafoods are very quick to cook, so are perfect for that impromptu occasion.

~~~~~~~~~~~~~~~

Sharp Cumin Prawn Kebabs

If you use cooked prawns (shrimp) for this dish, just barbecue them until they are hot. You can use peeled or unpeeled prawns but large, unpeeled crevettes will look and taste particularly good. You can also use the marinade for scallops or other seafood.

Serves 4

	METRIC	IMPERIAL	AMERICAN
Cumin seeds	15 ml	1 tbsp	1 tbsp
Grated lemon rind	15 ml	1 tbsp	1 tbsp
Spring onion (scallion), finely chopped	1	1	1
Chopped fresh parsley	30 ml	2 tbsp	2 tbsp
Sugar	5 ml	1 tsp	1 tsp
Oil	60 ml	4 tbsp	4 tbsp
Lemon juice	45 ml	3 tbsp	3 tbsp
Salt and freshly ground black pepper			
Large raw prawns (jumbo shrimp)	450 g	1 lb	1 lb

1   Lightly brown the cumin seeds in a dry pan.

2   Crush the seeds and mix with the lemon rind, spring onion, parsley, sugar, oil and lemon juice. Season with salt and pepper. Rub over the prawns and leave to stand for about 2 hours.

3   Thread the prawns on to soaked wooden skewers and barbecue for about 10 minutes, turning regularly.

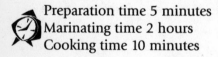

Preparation time 5 minutes
Marinating time 2 hours
Cooking time 10 minutes

Italian-style Prawn and Salami Kebabs

If you buy salami in a piece, cut it into chunks. If you only have sliced salami, roll the slices tightly into cylinders.

Serves 4

	METRIC	IMPERIAL	AMERICAN
Raw prawns (shrimp)	450 g	1 lb	1 lb
Salami	225 g	8 oz	½ lb
Salt and freshly ground black pepper			
Extra virgin olive oil	60 ml	4 tbsp	4 tbsp
Mozzarella cheese, sliced	225 g	8 oz	½ lb
Ripe tomatoes, sliced	4	4	4
Balsamic vinegar	15 ml	1 tbsp	1 tbsp
Chopped fresh basil	30 ml	2 tbsp	2 tbsp

1 Prepare the prawns as you like them: peeled, unpeeled or peeled but with the tails left on. Cut the salami into small chunks.

2 Thread the prawns and salami alternately on to soaked wooden skewers and season with salt and pepper. Brush with a little oil.

3 Barbecue the kebabs for about 5 minutes, turning frequently.

4 Arrange the cheese and tomatoes in overlapping rows in a flat serving dish and sprinkle with the remaining oil, the vinegar and basil. Season generously with pepper and a little salt. Place the kebabs on top to serve.

Preparation time 15 minutes
Cooking time 5 minutes

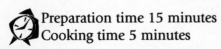

Scallop and Courgette Kebabs

Scallops freeze well so you can keep some ready for the weather to be right for your barbecue. Cut the courgettes into chunks about the same size as the scallops. You can make the sauce in advance and reheat it when you are almost ready to serve.

Serves 4

	METRIC	IMPERIAL	AMERICAN
Butter or margarine, melted	50 g	2 oz	¼ cup
Onions, chopped	2	2	2
Can of chopped tomatoes	400 g	14 oz	1 large
Chopped fresh basil	30 ml	2 tbsp	2 tbsp
Salt and freshly ground black pepper			
Shelled scallops	350 g	12 oz	¾ lb
Courgettes (zucchini), cut into chunks	2	2	2
Oil	15 ml	1 tbsp	1 tbsp

1 Heat the butter or margarine and fry (sauté) the onions until soft but not browned. Add the tomatoes and simmer gently for about 5 minutes. Stir in the basil and season with salt and pepper.

2 Thread the scallops and courgette chunks alternately on to soaked wooden skewers. Season with salt and pepper and brush with oil. Barbecue for about 10 minutes, turning and brushing with more oil if necessary.

3 Meanwhile, reheat the sauce to serve with the kebabs.

 Preparation time 10 minutes
Cooking time 15 minutes

Spiced Scallop and Mangetout Kebabs

Make the sauce in advance for this quick and tasty recipe.

Serves 4

	METRIC	IMPERIAL	AMERICAN
Oil	30 ml	2 tbsp	2 tbsp
Onion, finely chopped	1	1	1
Garlic cloves, crushed	2	2	2
Soy sauce	60 ml	4 tbsp	4 tbsp
Tomato purée (paste)	45 ml	3 tbsp	3 tbsp
Red wine vinegar	45 ml	3 tbsp	3 tbsp
Light brown sugar	30 ml	2 tbsp	2 tbsp
Ground ginger	2.5 ml	½ tsp	½ tsp
Chilli powder	2.5 ml	½ tsp	½ tsp
Shelled scallops	350 g	12 oz	¾ lb
Mangetout (snow peas)	225 g	8 oz	½ lb

1 Heat the oil and fry (sauté) the onion and garlic until soft but not browned. Add the soy sauce, tomato purée, vinegar, sugar, ginger and chilli, bring to the boil, then simmer for 3 minutes, stirring.

2 Thread the scallops and mangetout alternately on to soaked wooden skewers. Brush with the sauce.

3 Barbecue the kebabs for about 6 minutes, turning frequently and brushing with more sauce. Serve with any remaining sauce.

Preparation time 15 minutes
Cooking time 10 minutes

Toledo Tuna

Serves 4

	METRIC	IMPERIAL	AMERICAN
Can of anchovies	50 g	2 oz	1 small
A little milk			
Grated rind and juice of 1 lemon			
Chopped fresh parsley	15 ml	1 tbsp	1 tbsp
Chopped fresh thyme	15 ml	1 tbsp	1 tbsp
Garlic clove, crushed	1	1	1
Small onion, finely chopped	1	1	1
Olive oil	15 ml	1 tbsp	1 tbsp
Freshly ground black pepper			
Fresh tuna steaks, about 175 g/6 oz each	4	4	4
Mayonnaise (see page 134)	150 ml	¼ pt	⅔ cup
Green olives, stoned (pitted) and chopped	6	6	6
A little extra lemon juice (optional)			

1 Drain the oil from the can of anchovies into a shallow dish large enough to take the tuna steaks in a single layer. Put the anchovies in a small bowl and cover with milk.

2 Whisk the lemon rind and juice, the herbs, garlic, onion, olive oil and lots of black pepper into the anchovy oil. Add the tuna and turn to coat in the marinade. Leave to marinate for 1 hour.

3 Drain the anchovy fillets, discarding the milk, and chop very finely. Stir into the mayonnaise with the olives and sharpen with a little lemon juice, if liked.

4 Remove the tuna from the marinade and barbecue for about 5 minutes on each side until cooked through. Serve with the anchovy mayonnaise.

Preparation time 5 minutes
Marinating time 1 hour
Cooking time 10 minutes

Florida Haddock

An ideal recipe for any white fish

Serves 4

	METRIC	IMPERIAL	AMERICAN
Butter or margarine	*25 g*	*1 oz*	*2 tbsp*
Fillets of haddock or other white fish	*4*	*4*	*4*
Finely grated orange rind	*10 ml*	*2 tsp*	*2 tsp*
Finely grated grapefruit rind	*10 ml*	*2 tsp*	*2 tsp*
Freshly grated nutmeg			
Salt and freshly ground black pepper			

1 Grease the shiny side of four squares of foil with half the butter or margarine and sprinkle with half the grated rinds and a little nutmeg.

2 Season the fish on both sides with salt and pepper and lay the fish on the foil. Sprinkle with the remaining rind and a little more nutmeg. Dot with the remaining butter. Close the foil parcels.

3 Barbecue the parcels for about 25 minutes until the fish is cooked.

Preparation time 10 minutes
Cooking time 25 minutes

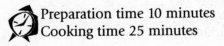

Mango Salsa Mackerel

Use canned mango if you don't have fresh.

Serves 4

	METRIC	IMPERIAL	AMERICAN
Mackerel, cleaned	4	4	4
Lime juice	90 ml	6 tbsp	6 tbsp
Lemon juice	15 ml	1 tbsp	1 tbsp
Salt and freshly ground black pepper			
Oil			
For the salsa:			
Mango, peeled and finely chopped	1	1	1
Red onion, finely chopped	1	1	1
Fresh green chilli, seeded and chopped	1	1	1
Chopped fresh coriander (cilantro)	15 ml 1	tbsp	1 tbsp
A few drops of Tabasco sauce			

1 Slash the mackerel diagonally through the skin three or four times on each side. Place in a shallow dish, pour over half the lime and all the lemon juice. Season with salt and pepper. Leave to marinate for at least 1 hour.

2 Mix together the salsa ingredients with the remaining lime juice.

3 Brush the fish with oil and barbecue for about 6–8 minutes on each side, depending on size. Serve with the mango salsa.

Preparation time 10 minutes
Marinating time 1 hour
Cooking time 16 minutes

Marmalade Mackerel

Try this with herring, too. The fish can also be cooked in foil parcels.

Serves 4

	METRIC	IMPERIAL	AMERICAN
Mackerel, cleaned	4	4	4
Orange marmalade	100 g	4 oz	⅓ cup
Butter or margarine, melted	50 g	2 oz	¼ cup
Salt and freshly ground black pepper			
Fine oatmeal	45 ml	3 tbsp	3 tbsp
Chopped fresh parsley	15 ml	1 tbsp	1 tbsp
To serve:			
Orange slices			

1 Spoon the marmalade inside the cavity of the fish and secure with cocktail sticks (toothpicks).

2 Brush the fish generously with butter or margarine. Season with salt and pepper and dust with oatmeal.

3 Barbecue in a hinged wire grille for about 8–10 minutes until cooked through and crisp.

4 Sprinkle with parsley and serve with orange slices.

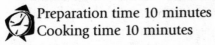
Preparation time 10 minutes
Cooking time 10 minutes

Roughy with Hot Sauce

Roughy is widely available in fishmongers, but you can substitute cod, monkfish or other firm white fish. Make the sauce hotter by adding more Tabasco sauce if you like.

Serves 4

	METRIC	IMPERIAL	AMERICAN
Chilli powder	1.5 ml	¼ tsp	¼ tsp
Pinch of dried thyme			
Butter or margarine, softened	40 g	1½ oz	3 tbsp
Roughy fillets	550 g	1¼ lb	1¼ lb
Salt and freshly ground black pepper			
For the sauce:			
Tabasco sauce	15 ml	1 tbsp	1 tbsp
Spring onions (scallions), finely chopped	3	3	3
Plain yoghurt	375 ml	13 fl oz	1½ cups

1 Blend the chilli powder and thyme into the butter or margarine and brush half the butter over one side of the fish. Season with salt and pepper.

2 Barbecue for about 5 minutes on the buttered side, then brush the other side with the remaining butter, season with salt and pepper, turn and barbecue for a further 3 minutes until just cooked.

3 Meanwhile, stir the Tabasco sauce and spring onions into the yoghurt. Serve with the cooked fillets.

Preparation time 10 minutes
Cooking time 10 minutes

Mediterranean Sardines

You can make the sauce in advance, then the sardines take only a few minutes to cook and serve.

Serves 4

	METRIC	IMPERIAL	AMERICAN
For the sauce:			
Olive oil	90 ml	6 tbsp	6 tbsp
White wine vinegar	15 ml	1 tbsp	1 tbsp
Garlic cloves, crushed	2	2	2
Shallot, finely chopped	1	1	1
Chopped fresh basil	30 ml	2 tbsp	2 tbsp
Chopped fresh parsley	15 ml	1 tbsp	1 tbsp
Grated rind and juice of 1 lemon			
Dijon mustard	2.5 ml	½ tsp	½ tsp
To finish:			
Plain (all-purpose) flour	45 ml	3 tbsp	3 tbsp
Salt and freshly ground black pepper			
Sardines, cleaned	450 g	1 lb	1 lb

1 Make the sauce in advance: purée half the olive oil and all the remaining sauce ingredients together until well blended.

2 Season the flour with salt and pepper. Dip the sardines in the flour, then shake off any excess. Dip in the remaining olive oil.

3 Barbecue the sardines for about 3 minutes on each side until cooked through. Serve with the sauce.

 Preparation time 15 minutes
Cooking time 6 minutes

Salmon with Sesame Seeds

Salmon has such a wonderful texture that it is best served simply. Try the same recipe with trout. Use whatever salad leaves you have to hand: young spinach leaves are a good choice if you have them.

Serves 4

	METRIC	IMPERIAL	AMERICAN
Sesame seeds	75 ml	5 tbsp	5 tbsp
Salmon steaks	4	4	4
Oil	45 ml	3 tbsp	3 tbsp
Salt and freshly ground black pepper			
Bunch of watercress, trimmed	1	1	1
Salad leaves, torn in pieces	8	8	8
Spring onions (scallions), sliced	6	6	6
Olive oil	60 ml	4 tbsp	4 tbsp
Sesame oil	30 ml	2 tbsp	2 tbsp
Red wine vinegar	45 ml	3 tbsp	3 tbsp
Soy sauce	30 ml	2 tbsp	2 tbsp
Grated fresh root ginger	15 ml	1 tbsp	1 tbsp
Sugar	5 ml	1 tsp	1 tsp

1 Toast the sesame seeds in a dry pan until golden, shaking the pan regularly. This can be done in advance.

2 Brush the salmon with oil and season with salt and pepper. Barbecue for about 5 minutes on each side.

3 Reheat the sesame seeds on a foil parcel at the side of the barbecue.

4   Mix the watercress, salad leaves and spring onions together in a shallow serving bowl.

5   Whisk together the remaining ingredients, pour over the salad and toss well.

6   Arrange the salmon on the salad and serve garnished with the sesame seeds.

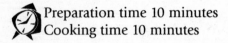
Preparation time 10 minutes
Cooking time 10 minutes

Salmon with Pesto

Serves 4

	METRIC	IMPERIAL	AMERICAN
Salmon steaks	4	4	4
Jar of pesto sauce	200 g	7 oz	1 small
Dry white wine	150 ml	¼ pt	⅔ cup

1   Place the salmon in a shallow bowl. Mix together the pesto sauce and wine and spoon over the fish, coating it well. Leave to marinate for 1 hour.

2   Barbecue the salmon for about 8 minutes on each side, basting with more sauce as it cooks.

3   Serve with any remaining sauce on the side.

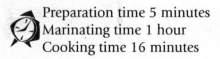
Preparation time 5 minutes
Marinating time 1 hour
Cooking time 16 minutes

Drunken Swordfish

Swordfish is now readily available in supermarkets and can be frozen successfully. However, if you don't have it, you can use any firm-fleshed fish steaks for this recipe, or even a meat steak. You can do everything in advance so that it is simple to cook on the barbecue.

Serves 4

	METRIC	IMPERIAL	AMERICAN
Bourbon or whisky	175 ml	6 fl oz	¾ cup
Fish or chicken stock	175 ml	6 fl oz	¾ cup
Groundnut (peanut) oil	75 ml	5 tbsp	5 tbsp
Garlic cloves, crushed	2	2	2
Salt and freshly ground black pepper			
Swordfish steaks	4	4	4

1 Mix together the bourbon or whisky, stock, oil and garlic and season very generously with salt and pepper.

2 Place the steaks in a glass or ceramic bowl, pour over the marinade, cover and leave to marinate for at least 1½ hours.

3 Drain the fish, season generously on both sides with salt and pepper and leave to stand until you are ready to cook.

4 Boil the marinade vigorously until it is reduced by half. Keep warm, or reheat at the side of the barbecue while the fish is cooking.

5 Barbecue the fish for about 10–15 minutes each side, depending on thickness, drizzling occasionally with the marinade.

Preparation time 5 minutes
Marinating time 1½ hours
Cooking time 20–30 minutes

~~~~~~~~~~~~~~

Lemon Tabasco Fish

Serves 4

	METRIC	IMPERIAL	AMERICAN
Fillets of cod or other white fish	4	4	4
Oil	120 ml	4 fl oz	½ cup
Lemon juice	45 ml	3 tbsp	3 tbsp
Tabasco sauce	5 ml	1 tsp	1 tsp
Spring onions (scallions)	8	8	8

1 Place the fish in a shallow dish. Mix together the oil, lemon juice and Tabasco sauce and pour over the fish. Leave to marinate for 1 hour.

2 Barbecue the fish for about 5 minutes on each side, depending on thickness, basting with more marinade while they cook.

3 Barbecue the spring onions for the last few minutes of cooking and serve with the fish.

Preparation time 5 minutes
Marinating time 1 hour
Cooking time 10 minutes

Sweet and Sour Seafood Kebabs

Use any firm-fleshed fish for this recipe: monkfish, red mullet and whiting are all good.

Serves 4

	METRIC	IMPERIAL	AMERICAN
Firm-fleshed fish	750 g	1½ lb	1½ lb
Onions, sliced into rings	2	2	2
Courgettes (zucchini), sliced into rings	3	3	3
Lemon, thinly sliced	1	1	1
Clear honey	60 ml	4 tbsp	4 tbsp
Lemon juice	30 ml	2 tbsp	2 tbsp
Soy sauce	15 ml	1 tbsp	1 tbsp
Pinch of chilli powder			

1 Cut the fish into large chunks, leaving the skin on.

2 Thread the fish, onions, courgettes and lemon alternately on to soaked wooden skewers. Lay the kebabs in a shallow dish.

3 Mix together the remaining ingredients and pour over the kebabs. Leave to marinate for 30 minutes.

4 Barbecue the kebabs for about 15 minutes, turning frequently and basting with the remaining marinade.

Preparation time 15 minutes
Marinating time 30 minutes
Cooking time 15 minutes

Pecan-stuffed Trout

Serves 4

	METRIC	IMPERIAL	AMERICAN
Even-sized trout, cleaned	4	4	4
Cooked long-grain rice	50 g	2 oz	¼ cup
Pecans, finely chopped	75 g	3 oz	¾ cup
Grated rind and juice of 1 lime			
Clear honey	5 ml	1 tsp	1 tsp
Chopped fresh parsley	30 ml	2 tbsp	2 tbsp
Salt and freshly ground black pepper			
Egg, beaten	1	1	1
A little oil			
To garnish:			
Lime wedges			

1 Rinse the trout and wipe with kitchen paper.

2 Mix the cooked rice with the nuts, lime rind and juice, honey and parsley. Season well with salt and pepper and mix with the beaten egg to bind.

3 Spoon into the body cavities of the fish and secure with cocktail sticks (toothpicks).

4 Brush all over with a little oil and barbecue for about 6–8 minutes on each side until cooked through. Serve garnished with lime wedges.

Preparation time 15 minutes
Cooking time 16 minutes

Halibut Parcels

Serves 4

	METRIC	IMPERIAL	AMERICAN
Dry white wine	150 ml	¼ pt	⅔ cup
Groundnut (peanut) oil	45 ml	3 tbsp	3 tbsp
Paprika	5 ml	1 tsp	1 tsp
Salt and freshly ground black pepper			
Clear honey	5 ml	1 tsp	1 tsp
Bay leaf	1	1	1
Chopped fresh parsley	15 ml	1 tbsp	1 tbsp
Snipped fresh chives	15 ml	1 tbsp	1 tbsp
Halibut steaks, 2.5 cm/1 in thick	4	4	4
Butter or margarine, melted	50 g	2 oz	¼ cup
Lemon juice	15 ml	1 tbsp	1 tbsp

1 Mix the first eight ingredients in a large, shallow dish.

2 Add the fish and turn to coat in the marinade. Leave to marinate for 1 hour, turning once.

3 Lay four large squares of foil, shiny side up, on the work surface. Brush liberally with the melted butter. Discard the bay leaf, then lay the fish on the foil. Drizzle with the remaining melted butter and the lemon juice. Season lightly again.

4 Wrap securely in the foil and barbecue for 15 minutes, turning once. Open the foil and cook for a further 5 minutes.

Preparation time 5 minutes
Marinating time 1 hour
Cooking time 20 minutes

MEAT

The best cuts of meat to use for barbecuing are the prime cuts, as these remain tender when cooked quickly, although cheaper cuts are fine if you have time to marinate them. Prepare meat carefully before you start, trimming off any fat that may drip on to the fire and cause flare-ups, and cutting the meat into similar-sized pieces so that it cooks evenly. Position meat at a suitable distance from the heat so that it has time to cook through to the centre while it browns nicely on the outside. If you place the meat too near the heat, it could burn on the outside before it is cooked through. Beef and lamb can be left rare on the inside, but pork must always be thoroughly cooked.

Sesame Beef

Serves 4

	METRIC	IMPERIAL	AMERICAN
Sesame seeds	30 ml	2 tbsp	2 tbsp
Garlic cloves, crushed	3	3	3
Dry white wine	120 ml	4 fl oz	1½ cups
Soy sauce	75 ml	5 tbsp	5 tbsp
Red wine vinegar	10 ml	2 tsp	2 tsp
Sesame oil	10 ml	2 tsp	2 tsp
Salt and freshly ground black pepper			
Good-quality steak, such as rump	450 g	1 lb	1 lb

1 Toast the sesame seeds in a dry pan until golden.

2 Mix the seeds with the garlic, wine, soy sauce, vinegar and sesame oil and season with salt and pepper.

3 Cut the steak into thin strips about 3 × 1 cm/ 1¼ × ½ in.

4 Marinate the steak in the mixture for 2 hours.

5 Thread the steak on to soaked wooden skewers and barbecue for about 5 minutes, turning occasionally.

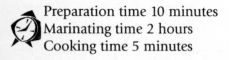
Preparation time 10 minutes
Marinating time 2 hours
Cooking time 5 minutes

Quick Burgers

Home-made burgers are more crumbly than the shop-bought variety, so cook in a hinged wire grille if you have one.

Serves 4

	METRIC	IMPERIAL	AMERICAN
Minced (ground) beef, lamb or pork	450 g	1 lb	4 cups
Onion, chopped	1	1	1
Garlic clove, crushed	1	1	1
Mustard powder	5 ml	1 tsp	1 tsp
Tomato purée (paste)	5 ml	1 tsp	1 tsp
Worcestershire sauce	5 ml	1 tsp	1 tsp
Salt and freshly ground black pepper			
Egg, beaten	1	1	1

1 Mix together the meat, onion, garlic, mustard, tomato purée and Worcestershire sauce, seasoning to taste with salt and pepper. Bind the mixture with the egg; you may not need to use all of it.

2 Press the mixture together firmly into patties and chill before cooking.

3 Barbecue for about 6 minutes on each side, depending on thickness, until cooked through.

Preparation time 10 minutes
Cooking time 12 minutes

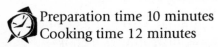

Cumin Kebabs

Discover one of the subtle flavours of the Middle East in this simple recipe.

Serves 4

	METRIC	IMPERIAL	AMERICAN
Lean beef, cubed	450 g	1 lb	1 lb
Red wine vinegar	15 ml	1 tbsp	1 tbsp
Milk	45 ml	3 tbsp	3 tbsp
Ground ginger	15 ml	1 tbsp	1 tbsp
Ground coriander (cilantro)	5 ml	1 tsp	1 tsp
Ground turmeric	2.5 ml	½ tsp	½ tsp
Cumin seeds	2.5 ml	½ tsp	½ tsp
Lemon juice	5 ml	1 tsp	1 tsp
Salt and freshly ground black pepper			
Butter or margarine, melted	45 ml	3 tbsp	3 tbsp

1 Place the meat in a shallow bowl and sprinkle with vinegar.

2 Mix together all the remaining ingredients except the butter or margarine and pour over the meat. Toss well. Leave to marinate for 30 minutes.

3 Thread the meat on to soaked wooden skewers and brush with butter or margarine.

4 Barbecue for about 20 minutes, turning frequently and basting with butter or margarine as it cooks.

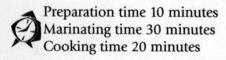

Preparation time 10 minutes
Marinating time 30 minutes
Cooking time 20 minutes

Pineapple Steaks

You can marinate the meat overnight if you have time.

Serves 4

	METRIC	IMPERIAL	AMERICAN
Fillet steaks	4	4	4
Can of pineapple in natural juice	410 g	14½ oz	1 large
Garlic cloves, crushed	2	2	2
Ground coriander (cilantro)	5 ml	1 tsp	1 tsp
Pinch of chilli powder			
Oil	60 ml	4 tbsp	4 tbsp
Salt and freshly ground black pepper			
Double (heavy) or whipping cream	30 ml	2 tbsp	2 tbsp

1   Arrange the steaks in a shallow dish.

2   Drain the pineapple. Coarsely purée the pineapple with the garlic, coriander and chilli. Pour over the steaks and leave to marinate for at least 2 hours, longer if possible.

3   Lift the steaks from the marinade and wipe off any excess. Brush with oil.

4   Barbecue the steaks for 5–8 minutes on each side until cooked to your liking. Season with salt and pepper.

5   Meanwhile, heat the marinade and stir in the cream.

6   Serve the steaks with the pineapple sauce.

Preparation time 10 minutes
Marinating time 2 hours
Cooking time 20 minutes

Beef with Creamy Walnut Sauce

Serves 4

	METRIC	IMPERIAL	AMERICAN
Walnuts, chopped	100 g	4 oz	1 cup
Spring onions (scallions), finely chopped	2	2	2
Chicken stock	60 ml	4 tbsp	4 tbsp
Lemon juice	45 ml	3 tbsp	3 tbsp
Ground ginger	1.5 ml	1/4 tsp	1/4 tsp
Salt and freshly ground black pepper			
Fromage frais	250 ml	8 fl oz	1 cup
Sirloin steak, cut into strips	450 g	1 lb	1 lb

1 Blend the walnuts, spring onions, stock, lemon juice, ginger, salt and pepper in a food processor or blender.

2 Thread the meat on to soaked wooden skewers. Brush generously with some of the walnut sauce. Mix the remaining sauce with the fromage frais.

3 Barbecue the kebabs for about 8 minutes on each side, turning frequently, until cooked to your liking.

4 Serve with the fromage frais sauce.

Preparation time 15 minutes
Cooking time 16 minutes

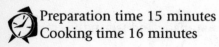

Steak with Peppers

Serves 4

	METRIC	IMPERIAL	AMERICAN
Garlic clove, crushed	1	1	1
Chopped fresh parsley	10 ml	2 tsp	2 tsp
Chopped fresh basil	10 ml	2 tsp	2 tsp
Oil	60 ml	4 tbsp	4 tbsp
Salt and freshly ground black pepper			
Frying steak, cut into wide strips	450 g	1 lb	1 lb
Red (bell) pepper, cut into thick strips	1	1	1
Green pepper, cut into thick strips	1	1	1
Yellow pepper, cut into thick strips	1	1	1
Onions, thickly sliced into rings	2	2	2

1 Mix the garlic, parsley and basil into the oil and season with salt and pepper. Brush over the steak, peppers and onions.

2 Barbecue the meat and vegetables for about 15 minutes until lightly browned on the outside, brushing frequently with the herb oil while cooking.

 Preparation time 15 minutes
Cooking time 15 minutes

Gammon Steaks in Ale

Serves 4

	METRIC	IMPERIAL	AMERICAN
Gammon steaks	4	4	4
Bitter or brown ale	300 ml	½ pt	1¼ cups
Onions, sliced	4	4	4
Bay leaf	1	1	1
Salt and freshly ground black pepper			
Black treacle (molasses)	60 ml	4 tbsp	4 tbsp
Lemon juice	15 ml	1 tbsp	1 tbsp
Oil	30 ml	2 tbsp	2 tbsp

1 Snip the steaks all round the edges to prevent curling. Place in a shallow dish. Mix together the beer, onions, bay leaf, salt and pepper, pour over the meat and marinate for at least 2 hours.

2 Lift the meat from the marinade, then strain the onions and reserve.

3 Boil the marinade vigorously until reduced by half. Stir in the treacle.

4 Heat the oil and fry (sauté) the strained onions until soft and golden brown.

5 Brush the gammon with the reduced marinade and barbecue for about 20 minutes, turning and basting with the marinade during cooking.

6 Cover with the fried onions and any remaining marinade to serve.

Preparation time 10 minutes
Marinating time 2 hours
Cooking time 20 minutes

Bratwurst with Tomato and Herb Sauce

Any good-quality frying sausages can be used for this dish.

Serves 4

	METRIC	IMPERIAL	AMERICAN
Passata (sieved tomatoes)	400 ml	14 fl oz	1¾ cups
Garlic cloves, crushed	2	2	2
Dried oregano	5 ml	1 tsp	1 tsp
Dried rosemary	5 ml	1 tsp	1 tsp
Salt and freshly ground black pepper			
Bratwurst or good-quality sausages	450 g	1 lb	1 lb

1 Mix together the passata, garlic, oregano, rosemary, salt and pepper. Brush over the sausages.

2 Barbecue the sausages for about 15–20 minutes, turning regularly and brushing with more sauce.

3 Meanwhile, heat the remaining sauce to serve with the sausages.

Preparation time 5 minutes
Cooking time 20 minutes

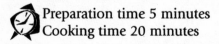

Allspice Pork

Use chops or cutlets for this recipe.

Serves 4

	METRIC	IMPERIAL	AMERICAN
Oil	15 ml	1 tbsp	1 tbsp
Small onion, finely chopped	1	1	1
Light brown sugar or honey	15 ml	1 tbsp	1 tbsp
Ground allspice	15 ml	1 tbsp	1 tbsp
Ground cinnamon	5 ml	1 tsp	1 tsp
Dried thyme	2.5 ml	½ tsp	½ tsp
Salt and freshly ground black pepper			
Pork chops	4	4	4
Treacly Apple Sauce (see page 36)			

1 Mix together the oil, onion, allspice, cinnamon, thyme, salt and pepper.

2 Rub the mixture over the pork on all sides. Leave to marinate for 2 hours.

3 Barbecue the pork for about 15 minutes on each side until thoroughly cooked through and crisp and golden brown on the edges.

4 Meanwhile, warm through the apple sauce to serve with the pork.

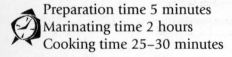
Preparation time 5 minutes
Marinating time 2 hours
Cooking time 25–30 minutes

Pork Escalope Pockets

You can also try this with turkey or veal.

Serves 4

	METRIC	IMPERIAL	AMERICAN
Pork escalopes	4	4	4
Paprika	*5 ml*	*1 tsp*	*1 tsp*
Salt and freshly ground black pepper			
Tomato ketchup (catsup)	*60 ml*	*4 tbsp*	*4 tbsp*
Slices of Emmenthal (Swiss) or strong hard cheese	*100 g*	*4 oz*	*¼ lb*
Finely snipped fresh chives	*30 ml*	*2 tbsp*	*2 tbsp*
Oil	*15 ml*	*1 tbsp*	*1 tbsp*

1 Beat the escalopes flat. Season with paprika, salt and pepper and brush with ketchup.

2 Place a slice of cheese on one half of each escalope and sprinkle with chives. Fold over and secure with cocktail sticks (toothpicks). Brush with oil.

3 Barbecue for about 8 minutes on each side, brushing with more oil if necessary.

Preparation time 10 minutes
Cooking time 16 minutes

Pork and Pineapple Grills

Serves 4

	METRIC	IMPERIAL	AMERICAN
Lean minced (ground) pork	450 g	1 lb	1 lb
Onion salt	2.5 ml	½ tsp	½ tsp
Freshly ground black pepper			
Dried sage	5 ml	1 tsp	1 tsp
Soy sauce	5 ml	1 tsp	1 tsp
Can of pineapple rings in natural juice	225 g	8 oz	1 small
Tomato purée (paste)	45 ml	3 tbsp	3 tbsp
Clear honey	45 ml	3 tbsp	3 tbsp
Worcestershire sauce	10 ml	2 tsp	2 tsp

1 Mix the minced pork with the onion salt, a good grinding of pepper, the sage and soy sauce. Shape into four round cakes.

2 Drain the pineapple, reserving the juice and press a pineapple ring firmly into each cake.

3 Blend a little of the pineapple juice with the tomato purée in a small saucepan until smooth. Then blend in the remaining juice, the honey and Worcestershire sauce. Bring to the boil and boil for 2–3 minutes.

4 Brush over the cakes and barbecue for about 10 minutes until glazed and cooked through, turning and brushing with the marinade during cooking.

Preparation time 10 minutes
Cooking time 10 minutes

Lamb with Curry Butter

You can also use this butter with chicken or any vegetables.

Serves 4

	METRIC	IMPERIAL	AMERICAN
Unsalted butter, softened	100 g	4 oz	½ cup
Spring onions (scallions), chopped	4	4	4
Curry powder	15 ml	1 tbsp	1 tbsp
Lemon juice	10 ml	2 tsp	2 tsp
Lamb cutlets or chops	4	4	4
Salt and freshly ground black pepper			

1 Purée the butter, spring onions, curry powder and lemon juice until smooth. Season to taste with salt and pepper. Chill, if possible.

2 Season the meat with salt and pepper and brush generously with the butter.

3 Barbecue for about 8 minutes on each side, brushing frequently with the flavoured butter.

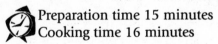
Preparation time 15 minutes
Cooking time 16 minutes

Lamb Armagnac

Use large lamb chops or cutlets.

Serves 4

	METRIC	IMPERIAL	AMERICAN
Coarsely grated rind and juice of 1 orange			
Chopped fresh basil	15 ml	1 tbsp	1 tbsp
Pinch of dried oregano			
Freshly ground black pepper			
Lamb chops	4	4	4
Armagnac or brandy	45 ml	3 tbsp	3 tbsp

1 Mix the orange juice, basil, oregano and pepper. Pour over the chops and leave to marinate for 1 hour.

2 Barbecue for 5–8 minutes on each side until cooked to taste, basting with any remaining marinade.

3 Place on a serving dish, spoon over the Armagnac or brandy and sprinkle with orange rind.

Preparation time 5 minutes
Marinating time 1 hour
Cooking time 15 minutes

Crusted Lamb Cutlets

Lamb is best cooked so that it is browned on the outside and remains just slightly pink and succulent on the inside.

Serves 4

	METRIC	IMPERIAL	AMERICAN
Fresh breadcrumbs	50 g	2 oz	1 cup
Dried marjoram	2.5 ml	½ tsp	½ tsp
Dried rosemary	2.5 ml	½ tsp	½ tsp
Salt and freshly ground black pepper			
Dry sherry	15 ml	1 tbsp	1 tbsp
Oil	30 ml	2 tbsp	2 tbsp
Lamb cutlets	4	4	4

1 Mix together the breadcrumbs, marjoram, rosemary, salt and pepper. Stir in the sherry and enough oil to moisten the mixture.

2 Brush the cutlets with oil, then press on the breadcrumb mixture.

3 Barbecue the cutlets for about 5–7 minutes on each side, depending on thickness, until cooked to your liking.

Preparation time 10 minutes
Cooking time 15 minutes

Lamb Kebabs with Spiced Apricots

Serves 4

	METRIC	IMPERIAL	AMERICAN
Lean lamb, cubed	450 g	1 lb	1 lb
Ready-to-eat dried apricots	300 g	11 oz	2 cups
Oil	75 ml	5 tbsp	5 tbsp
Salt and freshly ground black pepper			
For the sauce:			
Onion, sliced	1	1	1
Sultanas (golden raisins)	50 g	2 oz	1/3 cup
Desiccated (shredded) coconut	50 g	2 oz	1/2 cup
White wine vinegar	60 ml	4 tbsp	4 tbsp
Apricot jam (conserve) or apply jelly (clear conserve)	60 ml	4 tbsp	4 tbsp
Lemon juice	45 ml	3 tbsp	3 tbsp
Cayenne	15 ml	1 tbsp	1 tbsp

1 Thread the lamb and 225 g/8 oz/1⅓ cups of the apricots on to soaked wooden skewers. Brush with oil and season well with salt and pepper.

2 To make the sauce, heat 30 ml/2 tbsp of the remaining oil and fry (sauté) the onion until soft but not browned. Chop the remaining apricots and add with the sultanas and coconut. Stir over a low heat until well mixed.

3 Add the vinegar, jam or jelly and simmer for 2 minutes, stirring continuously.

4 Add the lemon juice and cayenne and season to taste with salt and pepper.

5 Barbecue the lamb for about 6 minutes on each side, turning regularly and brushing with more oil.

6 Reheat the sauce and serve with the lamb.

Preparation time 15 minutes
Cooking time 16 minutes

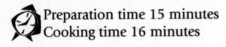

Rosé Lamb

Serves 4

	METRIC	IMPERIAL	AMERICAN
Lamb steaks	4	4	4
Sprigs of fresh rosemary	2	2	2
Rosé wine	150 ml	¼ pt	⅔ cup
Lemon juice	150 ml	¼ pt	⅔ cup
Oil	150 ml	¼ pt	⅔ cup
Garlic cloves, crushed	3	3	3
Salt and freshly ground black pepper			

1 Place the lamb in a shallow dish with the rosemary. Pour over the wine, lemon juice, oil, garlic, salt and pepper and marinate for 2 hours.

2 Barbecue the lamb for about 8 minutes on each side, depending on thickness, until cooked to your liking, basting frequently with the marinade during cooking.

Preparation time 5 minutes
Marinating time 2 hours
Cooking time 16 minutes

Mustard Rosemary Lamb

You may need eight lamb chops if they are very small. The same rub can be used on firm fish such as swordfish, or on chicken.

Serves 4

	METRIC	IMPERIAL	AMERICAN
Chopped fresh rosemary	60 ml	4 tbsp	4 tbsp
Garlic clove, crushed	1	1	1
Mustard powder	5 ml	1 tsp	1 tsp
Dried oregano	5 ml	1 tsp	1 tsp
Pinch of cayenne			
Salt and freshly ground black pepper			
Lamb cutlets or chops	4	4	4
Oil	30 ml	2 tbsp	2 tbsp

1 Blend or pound together the rosemary, garlic, mustard, oregano, cayenne, salt and pepper.

2 Rub well into the lamb cutlets or chops on all sides, then leave to stand for about 2 hours.

3 Brush with oil and barbecue over a medium heat for about 8 minutes on each side.

 Preparation time 5 minutes
Marinating time 2 hours
Cooking time 16 minutes

POULTRY

Chicken is a wonderfully versatile food which is perfect for barbecuing. Cooking it in its skin helps to retain the succulence of the meat and creates a delicious crispy coating. Always make sure that all poultry is thoroughly cooked. Avoid pricking the meat while cooking as the juices will seep out and make the meat dry. Just test the meat when you think it is ready; the juices from the thickest part should run clear when pierced.

Chicken Fajitas

This is good served with guacamole (see page 46) and a chilli relish.

Serves 4

	METRIC	IMPERIAL	AMERICAN
Onion, finely chopped	1	1	1
Garlic clove, crushed	1	1	1
Light brown sugar	75 g	3 oz	⅓ cup
Lager	300 ml	½ pt	1¼ cups
Red wine vinegar	60 ml	4 tbsp	4 tbsp
Made mustard	15 ml	1 tbsp	1 tbsp
Chicken breasts, cut into strips	4	4	4
Oil			
Salt and freshly ground black pepper			
Onion, sliced into rings	1	1	1
Red (bell) pepper, cut into thick strips	1	1	1
Green pepper, cut into thick strips	1	1	1
Flour tortillas	8	8	8

1 Place the onion, garlic, sugar, lager, vinegar and mustard in a pan, bring to the boil, then simmer for 5 minutes, stirring occasionally.

2 Place the chicken in a shallow bowl, pour over the sauce and leave to marinate for 1 hour.

3 Remove the chicken from the marinade, brush with oil and season with salt and pepper. Barbecue on foil for about 10 minutes on each side until cooked through.

4 Meanwhile, brush the onion rings and peppers with oil and barbecue for about 4 minutes on each side. Warm the tortillas at the side of the barbecue.

5 Lay the chicken, onion and peppers on the tortillas. Roll up and eat with your fingers.

Preparation time 10 minutes
Marinating time 1 hour
Cooking time 20 minutes

Chicken with Hot Olive Sauce

The chicken skin will crisp and blacken slightly for a wonderful taste. Make the sauce in advance, if liked.

Serves 4

	METRIC	IMPERIAL	AMERICAN
Chicken portions	4	4	4
For the sauce:			
Olive oil	60 ml	4 tbsp	4 tbsp
Onion, finely chopped	1	1	1
Garlic cloves, crushed	2	2	2
Green (bell) pepper, chopped	1	1	1
Can of chopped tomatoes	400 g	14 oz	1 large
Stoned (pitted) green olives, chopped	175 g	3 oz	½ cup
Cayenne	2.5 ml	½ tsp	½ tsp
A few drops of Worcestershire sauce			
Salt and freshly ground black pepper			

1 Wipe the chicken and brush with a little oil.

2 Make the sauce. Heat 30 ml/2 tbsp of the oil and fry (sauté) the onion, garlic and pepper until soft but not browned. Add the remaining sauce ingredients and simmer gently for 10 minutes.

3 Barbecue the chicken for 20–30 minutes, turning frequently and brushing with more oil as needed.

4 Meanwhile, reheat the sauce if necessary, either on the cooker or at the side of the barbecue.

Preparation time 10 minutes
Cooking time 30 minutes

Apple Chicken

Serves 4

	METRIC	IMPERIAL	AMERICAN
Chicken breasts or portions	4	4	4
Small onion, finely chopped	½	½	½
Garlic clove, crushed	1	1	1
Light brown sugar	15 ml	1 tbsp	1 tbsp
Made mustard	15 ml	1 tbsp	1 tbsp
Oil	15 ml	1 tbsp	1 tbsp
Apple juice	250 ml	8 fl oz	1 cup
Cider vinegar	120 ml	4 fl oz	½ cup
Paprika	15 ml	1 tbsp	1 tbsp
Chilli powder	5 ml	1 tsp	1 tsp
Salt and freshly ground black pepper			

1 Arrange the chicken pieces in a shallow dish. Mix together all the remaining ingredients and pour over the chicken. Leave to marinate for 2 hours.

2 Lift the chicken from the marinade. Boil the remaining marinade until reduced slightly.

3 Barbecue the chicken for about 20 minutes – chicken breasts will cook more quickly, larger portions will take longer – using the remaining marinade to brush the chicken as it cooks. Make sure the chicken is thoroughly cooked through before serving.

Preparation time 10 minutes
Marinating time 2 hours
Cooking time 20 minutes

Thai Chicken and Coconut

Serves 4

	METRIC	IMPERIAL	AMERICAN
Chicken breasts, cut into chunks	4	4	4
Lime juice	250 ml	8 fl oz	1 cup
Canned unsweetened coconut milk	250 ml	8 fl oz	1 cup
Peanut butter	100 g	4 oz	½ cup
Light brown sugar	50 g	2 oz	¼ cup
White wine vinegar	45 ml	3 tbsp	3 tbsp
Cornflour (cornstarch)	15 ml	1 tbsp	1 tbsp
Curry powder	5 ml	1 tsp	1 tsp
Oil	30 ml	2 tbsp	2 tbsp
Desiccated (shredded) coconut	30 ml	2 tbsp	2 tbsp

1 Marinate the chicken in the lime juice for 1 hour.

2 Blend the coconut milk, peanut butter, sugar, vinegar, cornflour and curry powder. Bring gently to the boil, stirring, then simmer for 3 minutes.

3 Drain the chicken and thread on to soaked wooden skewers. Brush with oil.

4 Barbecue the kebabs for about 10 minutes until the chicken is cooked through, turning frequently.

5 Reheat the sauce, pour over the kebabs and garnish with coconut.

Preparation time 5 minutes
Marinating time 1 hour
Cooking time 10 minutes

Lemon Chicken with Herbs

Use a combination of two or three fresh herbs, choosing from what you have to hand. Parsley, thyme, basil, rosemary, marjoram and oregano are all good choices.

Serves 4

	METRIC	IMPERIAL	AMERICAN
Chicken breasts	4	4	4
Olive oil	75 ml	5 tbsp	5 tbsp
Salt and freshly ground black pepper			
Chopped fresh herbs	50 g	2 oz	½ cup
Lemon juice	90 ml	6 tbsp	6 tbsp

1 Rub the chicken with a little oil, then season with salt and pepper.

2 Barbecue the chicken for about 7–8 minutes on each side until the skin is crispy and the flesh is almost cooked through.

3 Whisk together the remaining oil, the herbs and lemon juice. Brush over the chicken and continue to barbecue for another 3–4 minutes until thoroughly cooked.

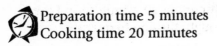
Preparation time 5 minutes
Cooking time 20 minutes

Barbecued Spatchcock Chicken

Serves 4

	METRIC	IMPERIAL	AMERICAN
Poussins	4	4	4
Mustard powder	5 ml	1 tsp	1 tsp
Butter or margarine, melted	40 g	1½ oz	3 tbsp
Worcestershire sauce	15 ml	1 tbsp	1 tbsp
Red wine vinegar	10 ml	2 tsp	2 tsp
Clear honey	5 ml	1 tsp	1 tsp

1 Split each poussin down the backbone and open out flat. Push a skewer through the legs of each to hold them flat.

2 Mix the remaining ingredients together and brush all over the poultry.

3 Barbecue, turning several times and brushing with the basting mixture, for about 30 minutes or until tender and cooked through.

4 Remove the skewers before serving.

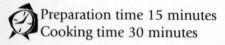
Preparation time 15 minutes
Cooking time 30 minutes

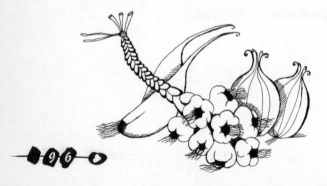

Chicken with Brandy and Orange Cream Sauce

Serves 4

	METRIC	IMPERIAL	AMERICAN
Chicken breasts	4	4	4
Oil	30 ml	2 tbsp	2 tbsp
Salt and freshly ground black pepper			
Butter or margarine, melted	100 g	4 oz	½ cup
Double (heavy) or whipping cream	90 ml	6 tbsp	6 tbsp
Brandy	60 ml	4 tbsp	4 tbsp
Orange juice	30 ml	2 tbsp	2 tbsp
Egg	1	1	1

1 Brush the chicken breasts with oil and season with salt and pepper.

2 Barbecue for about 10 minutes on each side until cooked through and crisp.

3 Meanwhile, whisk together all the remaining ingredients and warm through gently, seasoning to taste with salt and pepper. Serve the sauce with the chicken.

Preparation time 10 minutes
Cooking time 30 minutes

Sweet and Spicy Duck

Serves 4

	METRIC	IMPERIAL	AMERICAN
Duck breast portions	4	4	4
Dry sherry	120 ml	4 fl oz	½ cup
Strong black tea	120 ml	4 fl oz	½ cup
Soy sauce	120 ml	4 fl oz	½ cup
Garlic clove, crushed	1	1	1
Oil	30 ml	2 tbsp	2 tbsp
Clear honey	30 ml	2 tbsp	2 tbsp
Ground cloves	5 ml	1 tsp	1 tsp
Salt and freshly ground black pepper			

1 Arrange the duck in a shallow dish.

2 Mix together the sherry, tea, soy sauce, garlic, oil, honey, cloves, salt and pepper. Pour over the duck and leave to marinate for 1 hour.

3 Drain the duck. Pour the marinade into a pan and boil until reduced by half.

4 Barbecue the duck for about 12 minutes on each side, depending on size, brushing regularly with the remaining marinade.

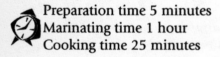
Preparation time 5 minutes
Marinating time 1 hour
Cooking time 25 minutes

VEGETABLES

Whole vegetables, vegetable slices, vegetable kebabs –
you can create all sorts of interesting main courses or
side dishes with wonderful colours, textures and
flavours on the barbecue.

~~~~~~~~~~

Courgette Ribbons Vinaigrette

Thread the courgette ribbons carefully for a very attractive effect.

Serves 4

	METRIC	IMPERIAL	AMERICAN
Courgettes (zucchini)	450 g	1 lb	1 lb
Olive oil	30 ml	2 tbsp	2 tbsp
White wine vinegar	5 ml	1 tsp	1 tsp
Garlic clove, crushed	1	1	1
Chopped fresh parsley	15 ml	1 tbsp	1 tbsp
Salt and freshly ground black pepper			

1 Use a potato peeler to cut long, thin ribbons off the courgettes. Place two or three ribbons on top of each other, then thread them on to soaked wooden skewers, folding them backwards and forwards like a concertina.

2 Whisk together the oil, vinegar, garlic, parsley, salt and pepper. Brush over the courgettes.

3 Barbecue for about 8–10 minutes, turning and basting frequently.

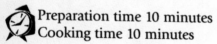
Preparation time 10 minutes
Cooking time 10 minutes

Fennel with Caraway

Par-boil the fennel in advance so that it is ready to cook quickly on the barbecue.

Serves 4

	METRIC	IMPERIAL	AMERICAN
Fennel bulbs, thickly sliced	4	4	4
Butter or margarine, melted	40 g	1½ oz	3 tbsp
Caraway seeds	15 ml	1 tbsp	1 tbsp
Salt and freshly ground black pepper			
Parmesan cheese, grated	50 g	2 oz	½ cup

1 Cook the fennel in boiling water for about 6 minutes until just tender. Drain well, then leave to cool.

2 Brush the fennel with butter, sprinkle with caraway seeds and season with salt and pepper.

3 Barbecue for about 2 minutes on each side until lightly browned.

4 Transfer to a serving dish and sprinkle with Parmesan.

 Preparation time 10 minutes
Cooking time 4 minutes

Leeks or Onions with Basil Butter

Serves 4

	METRIC	IMPERIAL	AMERICAN
Leeks or onions	4	4	4
Tomatoes, halved	4	4	4
Olive oil	30 ml	2 tbsp	2 tbsp
Garlic clove, crushed	1	1	1
Lemon juice	15 ml	1 tbsp	1 tbsp
Salt and freshly ground black pepper			
For the basil butter:			
Butter or margarine, softened	40 g	1½ oz	3 tbsp
Garlic clove, crushed	1	1	1
Chopped fresh basil	15 ml	1 tbsp	1 tbsp

1 Trim the leeks and cut them in half lengthways, or trim and halve the onions.

2 Brush the leeks or onions and tomatoes with olive oil, then barbecue the leeks for about 3 minutes on each side, or onions for about 6 minutes on each side until just soft and lightly browned, and the tomatoes for about 2 minutes.

3 Transfer to a serving dish and sprinkle with garlic, lemon juice, salt and pepper.

4 Meanwhile, blend the butter or margarine with the garlic and basil and season with salt and pepper. Dot over the vegetables and serve.

Preparation time 5 minutes
Cooking time 12 minutes

Mushroom and Banana Kebabs

Serves 4

	METRIC	IMPERIAL	AMERICAN
Button mushrooms	225 g	8 oz	½ lb
Red (bell) peppers, cut into chunks	2	2	2
Large courgette (zucchini), cut into chunks	1	1	1
Firm banana, cut into chunks	1	1	1
Salt and freshly ground black pepper			
Freshly grated nutmeg			
Butter or margarine, melted	50 g	2 oz	¼ cup

1 Thread the vegetables and banana alternately on to soaked wooden skewers.

2 Season with salt and pepper, sprinkle with nutmeg and brush well with butter or margarine.

3 Barbecue over a low heat (or near the edge of the barbecue) for about 15 minutes, brushing and basting regularly, until the pepper and courgette are tender.

Preparation time 10 minutes
Cooking time 15 minutes

Mixed Mushroom Kebabs

There are lots of different types of mushroom available now, so use a variety for extra interest. Try chestnut, oyster and field for example. Garlic bread (see page 126) makes a good accompaniment.

Serves 4

	METRIC	IMPERIAL	AMERICAN
Mixed large mushrooms	450 g	1 lb	1 lb
Olive oil	120 ml	4 fl oz	½ cup
Garlic clove, crushed	1	1	1
Salt and freshly ground black pepper			
Butter, melted	25 g	1 oz	2 tbsp
Dry sherry	30 ml	2 tbsp	2 tbsp
Chopped fresh flat-leaf parsley	30 ml	2 tbsp	2 tbsp

1 Toss the mushrooms in the oil with the garlic, a little salt and plenty of pepper until the oil is absorbed.

2 Thread the mushrooms on to soaked wooden skewers.

3 Barbecue the kebabs for about 8 minutes, turning frequently until crispy.

4 Meanwhile, mix together the butter, sherry and parsley and season with salt and pepper.

5 Arrange the kebabs in a shallow serving dish and pour over the flavoured butter.

Preparation time 15 minutes
Cooking time 8 minutes

Spiced Herb Onions

You can also use this basting mixture for other grilled vegetables.

Serves 4

	METRIC	IMPERIAL	AMERICAN
Small onions	45 g	1 lb	1 lb
For the basting mixture:			
Chopped fresh parsley	45 ml	3 tbsp	3 tbsp
Finely chopped spring onions (scallions)	3	3	3
Dried mixed herbs	5 ml	1 tsp	1 tsp
Mustard powder	2.5 ml	½ tsp	½ tsp
A few drops of chilli sauce			
Salt and freshly ground black pepper			
Butter or margarine, softened	225 g	8 oz	1 cup

1 Mix together the seasoning ingredients for the basting mixture and blend them into the butter or margarine. A food processor is a quick way to do this. Chill until ready to cook.

2 Brush the onions generously with the mixture, then continue to brush as you barbecue them for about 20 minutes until tender.

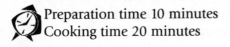

Preparation time 10 minutes
Cooking time 20 minutes

Chestnut Mushroom Parcels

Serves 4

	METRIC	IMPERIAL	AMERICAN
Chestnut mushrooms, sliced	450 g	1 lb	1 lb
Spring onions (scallions), chopped	2	2	2
Garlic cloves, crushed	2	2	2
Olive oil	60 ml	4 tbsp	4 tbsp
Balsamic vinegar	15 ml	1 tbsp	1 tbsp
Chopped fresh parsley	15 ml	1 tbsp	1 tbsp
Salt and freshly ground black pepper			
Tomatoes, halved	4	4	4
Chopped fresh basil	15 ml	1 tbsp	1 tbsp

1 Place the mushrooms in four squares of foil, shiny side up. Sprinkle with spring onions and garlic.

2 Whisk together 45 ml/3 tbsp of the oil with the vinegar, stir in the parsley and season with salt and pepper. Pour over the mushroom parcels and twist the foil at the top to seal.

3 Barbecue for about 15 minutes until cooked through.

4 Meanwhile, brush the tomatoes with the remaining oil, season with salt and pepper and barbecue for about 5 minutes until cooked.

5 Serve sprinkled with chopped basil.

Preparation time 10 minutes
Cooking time 15 minutes

Parsnip and Pears

Use skewers, if you find it easier, or just barbecue the fruit and vegetable pieces.

Serves 4

	METRIC	IMPERIAL	AMERICAN
Parsnips, cut into chunks	350 g	12 oz	³⁄₄ lb
Salt			
Firm pears, peeled and quartered	4	4	4
Butter or margarine	50 g	2 oz	¹⁄₄ cup
Light brown sugar	45 ml	3 tbsp	3 tbsp
Pinch of ground cinnamon			

1   Cook the parsnips in boiling salted water until just tender. Drain well.

2   Thread the parsnips and pears on to soaked wooden skewers, if preferred.

3   Blend together the butter or margarine, sugar and cinnamon. Brush over the kebabs.

4   Barbecue for about 4 minutes, turning several times and basting with more butter as they cook.

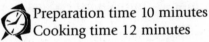
Preparation time 10 minutes
Cooking time 12 minutes

Parsnip and Pepper Kebabs

Use whatever colourful (bell) peppers you have available, cutting all the vegetables into even-sized pieces.

Serves 4

	METRIC	IMPERIAL	AMERICAN
Parsnip, cut into chunks	225g	8 oz	½ lb
Red (bell) pepper	1	1	1
Yellow pepper	1	1	1
Green pepper	1	1	1
Shallots	8	8	8
Small courgettes (zucchini), cut into chunks	4	4	4
For the dressing:			
Soy sauce	60 ml	4 tbsp	4 tbsp
Oil	15 ml	1 tbsp	1 tbsp
Lemon juice	15 ml	1 tbsp	1 tbsp
Ground ginger	2.5 ml	½ tsp	½ tsp
Clear honey	30 ml	2 tbsp	2 tbsp

1   Boil the parsnip for 3 minutes until almost cooked. Drain.

2   Cut the peppers into squares, blanch in boiling water for 3 minutes, then drain. Blanch the shallots in boiling water for about 5 minutes until just beginning to soften, then drain. Blanch the courgettes in boiling water for 2 minutes, then drain.

3   Thread all the vegetables alternately on to soaked wooden skewers.

4 Mix together the dressing ingredients and brush well over the kebabs.

5 Barbecue the kebabs for about 10 minutes, turning and basting frequently.

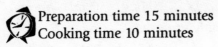

Preparation time 15 minutes
Cooking time 10 minutes

Red Onions with Bacon

Serves 4

	METRIC	IMPERIAL	AMERICAN
Red onions, cut into wedges	4	4	4
Streaky bacon rashers (slices), rinded and quartered	4	4	4
Oil	30 ml	2 tbsp	2 tbsp
Salt and freshly ground black pepper			
Chopped fresh parsley	15 ml	1 tbsp	1 tbsp

1 Thread the onions and bacon alternately on soaked wooden skewers. Brush with oil and season with salt and pepper.

2 Barbecue for about 10 minutes, turning frequently and brushing with more oil if necessary. Serve sprinkled with parsley.

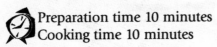

Preparation time 10 minutes
Cooking time 10 minutes

Herby Potato Parcels

Serves 4

	METRIC	IMPERIAL	AMERICAN
Butter or margarine	50 g	2 oz	¼ cup
Potatoes, scrubbed and thinly sliced	4	4	4
Chopped fresh parsley	15 ml	1 tbsp	1 tbsp
Snipped fresh chives	15 ml	1 tbsp	1 tbsp
Chopped fresh sage	5 ml	1 tsp	1 tsp
Salt and freshly ground black pepper			

1 Melt the butter or margarine in a large saucepan. Remove from the heat.

2 Add the sliced potatoes, herbs and a little salt and pepper and toss until each slice is coated.

3 Divide in a thin, even layer on four pieces of foil, shiny side up. Wrap securely and barbecue for about 20 minutes, turning occasionally until the potatoes are tender.

 Preparation time 10 minutes
Cooking time 20 minutes

Chilli-stuffed Peppers

Serves 4

	METRIC	IMPERIAL	AMERICAN
Green or red (bell) peppers	4	4	4
Mushrooms, finely chopped	50 g	2 oz	2 oz
Cheddar cheese, grated	75 g	3 oz	¾ cup
Can of red kidney beans, drained	425 g	15 oz	1 large
Tomato chilli salsa (ready-made)	60 ml	4 tbsp	4 tbsp
Ground cumin	2.5 ml	½ tsp	½ tsp
Dried oregano	5 ml	1 tsp	1 tsp
Garlic salt			
Freshly ground black pepper			

1 Cut a slice off the top of each pepper and remove and discard the seeds. Boil the peppers and 'lids' in lightly salted water for 6 minutes until just tender. Drain, rinse with cold water and drain again. Dry on kitchen paper.

2 Mix 50 g/2 oz/½ cup of the cheese with the remaining ingredients and spoon into the peppers. Top with the remaining cheese, then the 'lids'.

3 Wrap each securely in a double thickness of foil, shiny side in. Barbecue for about 30 minutes, turning occasionally, until piping hot and cooked through.

Preparation time 15 minutes
Cooking time 30 minutes

Vegetable Barbecue Ideas

* Wrap sweetcorn (corn) cobs in a slice of bacon or prosciutto, season and brush with butter or oil. Wrap in a square of foil and place on the side of the barbecue for about 45 minutes until tender.

* Blend some chopped fresh herbs and crushed garlic into softened butter or margarine to brush over vegetables as they cook.

* Brush small whole (bell) peppers with olive oil and barbecue until soft and scorched in places. Serve halved and seeded (pitted) with a little olive oil and coarse sea salt sprinkled over.

* If you put a selection of vegetables on one kebab skewer, make sure they are cut to similar sizes so that they will cook in about the same length of time. Intersperse them with pickles or sun-dried tomatoes in oil for added flavour.

* Par-boil almost any vegetables in large chunks, then dress in flavoured butter and brown on the barbecue or cook in foil packets.

* Slice courgettes (zucchini) in half lengthways, brush generously with olive oil and sprinkle with salt, pepper, a little crushed garlic and a little basil or oregano before placing on the barbecue. Treat peppers, onions or large mushrooms in the same way.

* Halve cooked jacket potatoes. Scoop out the flesh, season and mash with grated Cheddar, chopped onion and some chopped sage. Pile back in and heat on the side of the barbecue.

* Thread cherry tomatoes on soaked wooden skewers, brush with oil, then barbecue for a few minutes. Serve with herb butter (see page 38).

INTERESTING EXTRAS

You need some side dishes to go with your barbecued foods and it is usually best to prepare these in the kitchen and have them ready to serve when the main course from the barbecue is piping hot and ready. Here is a selection of simple vegetable, rice and grain dishes, breads and salads that offer interesting barbecue combinations. You can also use your conventional oven to keep foods warm, especially if you have a large number of guests and a relatively small barbecue. Preheat the oven to 160°C/325°F/gas mark 3 to make sure that foods stay hot without overcooking, but do keep an eye on the dishes to make sure they are still at their best. Place them on ovenproof serving plates and cover tightly with foil to retain the moisture before placing in the oven.

~~~~~~~~~~

Artichoke Cream

Serves 4

	METRIC	IMPERIAL	AMERICAN
Can of artichoke hearts, drained	400 g	14 oz	1 large
Mayonnaise (see page 134)	250 ml	8 fl oz	1 cup
Garlic clove, crushed	1	1	1
Chopped fresh basil	5 ml	1 tsp	1 tsp
White wine vinegar	5 ml	1 tsp	1 tsp
Salt and freshly ground black pepper			
Parmesan cheese, grated	75 g	3 oz	¾ cup
Fresh breadcrumbs	25 g	1 oz	½ cup

1 Preheat the oven to 200°C/400°F/gas mark 6.

2 Arrange the artichokes in a shallow ovenproof dish.

3 Mix together the mayonnaise, garlic, basil, vinegar, salt and pepper and pour over the artichokes.

4 Mix together the cheese and breadcrumbs and sprinkle over the top.

5 Bake in the oven for 20–25 minutes until golden.

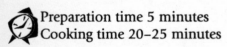 Preparation time 5 minutes
Cooking time 20–25 minutes

Celery and Beans in Soured Cream

Serves 4

	METRIC	IMPERIAL	AMERICAN
Celery sticks	6	6	6
French (green) beans, trimmed	450 g	1 lb	1 lb
Olive oil	60 ml	4 tbsp	4 tbsp
Soured (dairy sour) cream	150 ml	¼ pt	⅔ cup
Caraway seeds	15 ml	1 tbsp	1 tbsp
Salt and freshly ground black pepper			

1 Cut the celery into pieces the same size as the beans. Cook the celery in boiling water for 4 minutes, add the beans and cook for a further 2 minutes, then drain well.

2 Heat the oil and fry (sauté) the vegetables quickly for 2 minutes.

3 Stir in the soured cream and caraway seeds and season with salt and pepper.

Preparation time 10 minutes
Cooking time 15 minutes

Mushrooms in Balsamic Vinegar

Use almost any kind of mushrooms for this dish.

Serves 4

	METRIC	IMPERIAL	AMERICAN
Button mushrooms	450 g	1 lb	1 lb
Lemon juice	30 ml	2 tbsp	2 tbsp
Salt and freshly ground black pepper			
Balsamic vinegar	150 ml	¼ pt	⅔ cup
Olive oil	120 ml	4 fl oz	½ cup
Garlic cloves, crushed	4	4	4
Chopped capers	15 ml	1 tbsp	1 tbsp
Chopped fresh parsley	45 ml	3 tbsp	3 tbsp

1 Place the mushrooms and lemon juice in a pan and season with salt and pepper. Just cover with water, bring to the boil, then simmer for about 5 minutes until tender. Drain.

2 Meanwhile, bring the vinegar, oil and garlic to the boil in a separate pan. Simmer for 20 minutes.

3 Pour this hot marinade over the mushrooms, then leave to cool.

4 Add the capers and parsley and season to taste with salt and pepper.

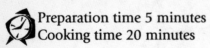
Preparation time 5 minutes
Cooking time 20 minutes

Sweet Glazed Shallots

Serves 4-6

	METRIC	IMPERIAL	AMERICAN
Small shallots	450 g	1 lb	1 lb
Butter or margarine, melted	50 g	2 oz	¼ cup
Golden (light corn) syrup	60 ml	4 tbsp	4 tbsp

1 Preheat the oven to 200°C/400°F/gas mark 6.

2 Peel the shallots, then place them in a pan, cover with water and bring to the boil. Simmer for 4 minutes, then drain thoroughly.

3 Arrange the shallots in a shallow ovenproof dish and pour over the butter or margarine. Drizzle with the syrup.

4 Cook in the oven for about 20 minutes, stirring occasionally, until the onions are tender and golden.

Preparation time 10 minutes
Cooking time 30 minutes

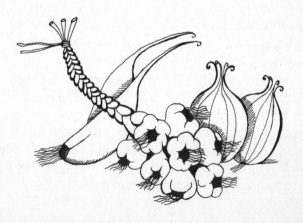

Potato Ideas

❋ The humble jacket potato is so easy and delicious, but
they take about 2 hours to cook on the barbecue,
depending on size, so pre-cook them to save time.
Pierce scrubbed potatoes with a fork and microwave on
high for about 3 minutes per potato. Rub with a little
coarse salt and oil, then wrap in foil. Alternatively,
season and wrap them and cook them in a hot oven at
200°C/400°F/gas mark 6 for about 1 hour. Place the
wrapped potatoes directly on the barbecue coals to
finish cooking.

❋ Serve crispy potato skins (see page 49) as a side dish
with a bowl of soured (dairy sour) cream flavoured
with snipped chives.

❋ Offer a selection of toppings for baked potatoes: grated
or crumbled cheese; chopped prawns (shrimp) in
mayonnaise (see page 134); chilli or bolognese sauce;
pats of herb butter (see page 38); pats of garlic butter –
as strong as you dare! (see page 38); anchovy butter
(see page 38); even hot baked beans.

❋ Peel and thinly slice potatoes and layer in an ovenproof dish, sprinkling each layer with salt, pepper and
your favourite herb as you go. Half-fill with milk, dot
with butter and bake in a preheated oven at 200°C/
400°F/gas mark 6 for about 50 minutes until the
potatoes are tender and the top browned.

❋ Peel potatoes and slice thickly, without cutting right
through to the base (much as you would to make
garlic bread). Slide a piece of bay leaf into each slit,
sprinkle with salt and pepper and brush with plenty of
olive oil. Bake in a preheated oven at 190°C/375°F/gas
mark 5 for about 1 hour, depending on the size of the
potatoes, until they are tender and golden brown.

Vegetable Ideas

✳ Especially if you have highly flavoured barbecued meats or vegetables, then steamed or boiled carrots, peas, broccoli, baby sweetcorn (corn), mangetout (snow peas), green beans or other vegetables in season (or from the freezer) are a tasty and colourful option, topped with a knob of butter.

✳ Ratatouille is a real barbecue favourite. You can buy ratatouille in cans and have one on standby, but it is not difficult to make and quantities are irrelevant as long as the finished result tastes good. Warm a little olive oil and fry (sauté) some sliced onions and garlic until soft, then add sliced (bell) peppers, courgettes (zucchini), aubergines (eggplants) and tomatoes or a can of tomatoes and simmer gently. Season well with salt and pepper and add some chopped fresh or dried herbs such as parsley and thyme.

✳ Another favourite is Courgettes Provençale: fry (sauté) some chopped onion and garlic in a little olive oil. Add a can of chopped tomatoes and simmer until pulpy. Add sliced courgettes and seasoning. Simmer until tender.

✳ A vegetable purée is another good option. Purée hot cooked peas, carrots, celeriac (celery root) or swede (rutabaga) with a little milk or cream and plenty of seasoning.

Wild Rice Salad

Wild rice takes longer to cook than white rice, but since it can be prepared in advance and does not need much attention, it is worth the extra time. You can buy wild rice mix too, which can be cooked in stock instead of water according to packet directions.

Serves 4

	METRIC	IMPERIAL	AMERICAN
Vegetable stock	450 ml	¾ pt	2 cups
Wild rice	100 g	4 oz	½ cup
Long-grain rice	175 g	6 oz	¾ cup
Can of red pimientos, drained and chopped	400 g	14 oz	1 large
Oil	60 ml	4 tbsp	4 tbsp
Red wine vinegar	30 ml	2 tbsp	2 tbsp
Worcestershire sauce	5 ml	1 tsp	1 tsp
Salt and freshly ground black pepper			

1 Bring the stock to the boil. Pour in the wild rice, return to the boil, cover and simmer gently for 35 minutes.

2 Add the long-grain rice, cover again and simmer for about 20 minutes until all the rice is cooked. If there is any liquid left, uncover and boil until absorbed. Leave to cool.

3 Stir in the pimientos.

4 Mix together the oil, vinegar, Worcestershire sauce, salt and pepper. Pour over the salad and toss together well.

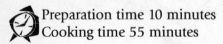
Preparation time 10 minutes
Cooking time 55 minutes

Rice Ideas

Rice can be used hot or cold, as the basis for a warming rice dish or an interesting salad.

* Make a simple rice salad by mixing cold, cooked long-grain rice with some cooked peas, toasted nuts and currants. Toss in a little French dressing to moisten.

* To make ginger and pepper fried rice: heat a little olive oil and gently soften some chopped onion, garlic and red and green (bell) pepper. Stir in some cooked long-grain rice and 5 ml/1 tsp grated fresh or minced (finely chopped) ginger and stir together until hot. Season with salt and pepper or soy sauce.

* If you are serving Eastern-inspired barbecued foods, choose a Chinese fried rice dish or Thai fragrant rice.

* If you like a simple side dish, cook rice in a chicken or vegetable stock to give it extra flavour.

* Add a finely pared lemon rind to the water when cooking rice, then sprinkle it with a little lemon juice and top with 5 ml/1 tsp grated lemon rind to serve.

Spiced Bulghar with Pine Nuts

You can serve this hot or cold.

Serves 4

	METRIC	IMPERIAL	AMERICAN
Olive oil	60 ml	4 tbsp	4 tbsp
Onions, finely chopped	2	2	2
Garlic clove, finely chopped	1	1	1
Pine nuts	30 ml	2 tbsp	2 tbsp
Bulghar wheat	150 g	5 oz	scant 1 cup
Salt and freshly ground black pepper			
Vegetable stock	600 ml	1 pt	2½ cups
Raisins	30 ml	2 tbsp	2 tbsp
Pinch of ground coriander (cilantro)			
Pinch of ground cinnamon			

1 Heat half the oil and gently fry (sauté) the onions until beginning to soften. Add the garlic and pine nuts and continue to fry until the onions are soft.

2 Stir in the bulghar and remaining oil, season with salt and pepper and stir well together.

3 Add the stock and remaining ingredients, cover and bring to the boil. Simmer for about 15 minutes until all the stock is absorbed.

4 If serving hot, stand the pan in a warm place or at the side of the barbecue for about 30 minutes until the bulghar is soft and swollen. Alternatively, leave to cool. Fluff up with a fork before serving.

Preparation time 5 minutes
Cooking time 1 hour

Classic Campfire Damper

Serves 4

	METRIC	IMPERIAL	AMERICAN
Self-raising (self-rising) flour	350 g	12 oz	3 cups
Salt	5 ml	1 tsp	1 tsp
Dried milk (non-fat milk powder)	15 ml	1 tbsp	1 tbsp
Butter or margarine	25 g	1 oz	2 tbsp
Water	300 ml	½ pt	1¼ cups

A little extra butter or margarine for greasing and
   flour for dusting

1   Mix the flour and salt with the dried milk.

2   Rub in the butter or margarine.

3   Quickly mix in the water with a knife until the
mixture forms a dough. Knead in the bowl for a few
minutes until smooth.

4   Shape into a round and place on a piece of greased
and floured foil, shiny side up.

5   Make a few slashes in the top with a knife, then wrap
loosely but securely in foil. Place in the hot coals and
cook for about 20 minutes until golden brown and
the base sounds hollow when tapped. Serve hot.

Preparation time 8 minutes
Cooking time 20 minutes

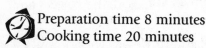

Pitta Packets

Make and wrap these in advance and keep them in the warming drawer if your barbecue has one. If you like the taste of ginger but can't be bothered with fresh, buy a jar of minced (finely chopped) ginger to keep in the fridge.

Serves 4

	METRIC	IMPERIAL	AMERICAN
Vegetable stock	300 ml	½ pt	1¼ cups
Leeks, sliced	225 g	8 oz	½ lb
Small apple, chopped	1	1	1
Radishes, chopped	6	6	6
Button mushrooms, sliced	4	4	4
Grated fresh root ginger	10 ml	2 tsp	2 tsp
Salt and freshly ground black pepper			
Olive oil	60 ml	4 tbsp	4 tbsp
White wine vinegar	15 ml	1 tbsp	1 tbsp
Pinch of mustard powder			
Pitta breads	4	4	4

1 Bring the stock to the boil in a pan, add the leeks and simmer for about 10 minutes until soft. Drain and cool.

2 Mix together the leeks, apple, radishes, mushrooms and ginger. Season with salt and pepper.

3 Blend together 45 ml/3 tbsp of the oil, the vinegar and mustard and sprinkle over the vegetables.

4 Slit the pitta breads lengthways down one side and fill with the vegetable mixture. Brush the outsides with the remaining oil and wrap the breads individually in foil.

5 Heat on the barbecue for about 6 minutes.

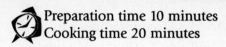 Preparation time 10 minutes
Cooking time 20 minutes

Crispy Fruit Coleslaw

Bought coleslaw is nothing like the real thing. Don't worry too much about quantities: add whatever you think makes a good balanced taste.

Serves 4–6

	METRIC	IMPERIAL	AMERICAN
Small white cabbage	1/2	1/2	1/2
Small onion, grated	1	1	1
Carrot, grated	1	1	1
Eating (dessert) apple, grated	1	1	1
Raisins or sultanas (golden raisins)	50 g	2 oz	1/3 cup
Mayonnaise (see page 134)	150 ml	1/4 pt	2/3 cup
A little milk			
Salt and freshly ground black pepper			

1 Shred the cabbage finely and place in a large bowl. Add the onion, carrot, apple and raisins or sultanas and mix well.

2 Thin the mayonnaise with a little milk and season with salt and pepper. Pour over the salad and toss together well.

 Preparation time 15 minutes

Bread Ideas

* When you are in a hurry, the last thing you are likely to think about is making bread – especially when there is no end of exciting breads available in the supermarkets and bakers. Serve two or three tasty breads with a barbecue to add variety and interest.

* French baguettes are great – but there are lots of other possibilities. Try some of the Mediterranean-style breads with olives or sun-dried tomatoes, Italian breads such as ciabatta or pugili, or warm pitta breads. Most of these freeze well.

* Wrap the bread in foil and warm it at the side of the barbecue to add that wonderful aroma of warm bread to the cooking.

* Rub a cut garlic clove over slices of baguette or crusty bread, then rub with the cut side of a ripe tomato (or with a tinned tomato) and sprinkle generously with olive oil, salt and freshly ground black pepper. Serve as a starter or with the meal.

* If all you have is some stale bread, don't despair. Slice it thinly and toast it, then cut it into fingers to make your own crisp melba toasts. Or cut it into squares or triangles and fry it in hot oil with a dried chilli to make delicious croûtons.

* Make garlic bread. Mash 100 g/4 oz/½ cup softened butter with 2 crushed garlic cloves and a little chopped fresh parsley. Cut a baguette in slices, not right through the base. Spread each slice with the garlic butter. Wrap in foil and bake in a preheated oven at 200°C/400°F/gas mark 6 for 14–20 minutes, or place at the edge of the barbecue and turn once or twice until hot and crisp.

Hot Lentil Salad

You can cook dried lentils in water with an onion and carrot for about 2 hours until tender, but canned lentils are a lot quicker and easier and taste just as good.

Serves 4

	METRIC	IMPERIAL	AMERICAN
Can of lentils	400 g	14 oz	1 large
Oil	45 ml	3 tbsp	3 tbsp
Streaky bacon, rinded, cut into chunks	175 g	6 oz	1 cup
Red wine vinegar	45 ml	3 tbsp	3 tbsp
Mild mustard	5 ml	1 tsp	1 tsp
Salt and freshly ground black pepper			
Chopped fresh parsley	15 ml	1 tbsp	1 tbsp

1 Warm the lentils gently in a pan.

2 Meanwhile, heat a little of the oil and fry (sauté) the bacon pieces until crisp.

3 Blend the remaining oil with the wine vinegar, mustard, salt and pepper to make a vinaigrette.

4 Drain the lentils, mix with the bacon and blend with the dressing. Season again with salt and pepper to taste. Sprinkle with parsley and serve hot.

Preparation time 5 minutes
Cooking time 10 minutes

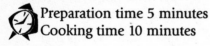

Aubergine Salad

Serves 4

	METRIC	IMPERIAL	AMERICAN
Tomatoes, cut into small wedges	2	2	2
Red (bell) pepper, cut into strips	1	1	1
Onion, cut into rings	1	1	1
White wine vinegar	30 ml	2 tbsp	2 tbsp
Dry sherry	30 ml	2 tbsp	2 tbsp
Oil	90 ml	6 tbsp	6 tbsp
Sesame oil	5 ml	1 tsp	1 tsp
Pinch of sugar			
Salt and freshly ground black pepper			
Aubergine (eggplant)	1	1	1
Lemon juice	30 ml	2 tbsp	2 tbsp

1 Mix the tomatoes, pepper and onion in a salad bowl.

2 Mix together the vinegar, sherry, 15 ml/1 tbsp of the oil, the sesame oil, sugar, salt and pepper. Pour over the salad and leave to marinate.

3 Cut the aubergine into thin strips and toss in lemon juice to prevent discolouring.

4 Heat the remaining oil and fry (sauté) the aubergine for about 8 minutes until lightly browned. Drain well and leave to cool.

5 Mix the aubergine into the salad and toss together gently.

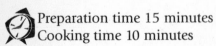
Preparation time 15 minutes
Cooking time 10 minutes

Red Cabbage Salad

Always toss apples in a little lemon juice as soon as you have sliced them to prevent them going brown.

Serves 4

	METRIC	IMPERIAL	AMERICAN
Red cabbage, finely shredded	225 g	8 oz	½ lb
Orange, peeled and cut into chunks	1	1	1
Eating (dessert) apple, chopped	1	1	1
Sultanas (golden raisins)	50 g	2 oz	⅓ cup
Orange juice	60 ml	4 tbsp	4 tbsp
Lemon juice	30 ml	2 tbsp	2 tbsp
Clear honey	15 ml	1 tbsp	1 tbsp
Oil	60 ml	4 tbsp	4 tbsp
Salt and freshly ground black pepper			
Banana	1	1	1

1 Mix together the cabbage, orange, apple and sultanas in a salad bowl.

2 Whisk together the orange and lemon juices, honey and oil. Season with salt and pepper. Pour over the salad and toss together well. Leave to stand for 2 hours.

3 Just before serving, slice the banana and add it to the salad. Toss again and adjust the seasoning to taste.

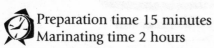

Preparation time 15 minutes
Marinating time 2 hours

Greek Potato Salad

Serves 4

	METRIC	IMPERIAL	AMERICAN
New potatoes, cooked and diced	450 g	1 lb	1 lb
Tomatoes, chopped	225 g	8 oz	½ lb
Onion, finely chopped	1	1	1
Black olives, stoned (pitted)	50 g	2 oz	⅓ cup
Mayonnaise (see page 134)	45 ml	3 tbsp	3 tbsp
Plain yoghurt	30 ml	2 tbsp	2 tbsp
Salt and freshly ground black pepper			

1 Carefully mix together the potatoes, tomatoes, onion and olives.

2 Mix together the mayonnaise and yoghurt and season with salt and pepper.

3 Pour the dressing over the salad and toss well. Chill before serving.

 Preparation time 10 minutes

Cucumber and Walnut Salad

Serves 4

	METRIC	IMPERIAL	AMERICAN
Cucumber, sliced	1	1	1
Radishes, thinly sliced	8	8	8
Green (bell) pepper, chopped	1	1	1
Spring onions (scallions), chopped	2	2	2
Walnuts, chopped	50 g	2 oz	½ cup
Chopped fresh parsley	15 ml	1 tbsp	1 tbsp
Chopped fresh thyme	5 ml	1 tsp	1 tsp
For the dressing:			
Soy sauce	60 ml	4 tbsp	4 tbsp
Oil	15 ml	1 tbsp	1 tbsp
Lemon juice	15 ml	1 tbsp	1 tbsp
Ground ginger	2.5 ml	½ tsp	½ tsp
Clear honey	15 ml	1 tbsp	1 tbsp
Water	60 ml	4 tbsp	4 tbsp

1 Mix together all the salad ingredients.

2 Whisk together the dressing ingredients.

3 Pour the dressing over the salad and toss together well.

 Preparation time 15 minutes

Salad Ideas

* Coarsely grate four or five carrots and season with lots of freshly ground black pepper, then dress in a simple vinaigrette dressing (see page 133); or with 45 ml/ 3 tbsp orange juice mixed with 15 ml/1 tbsp lemon juice; or with a yoghurt or fromage frais dressing (see page 134).

* Layer sliced tomatoes with a sprinkling of sugar and snipped fresh chives, then spoon over some vinaigrette dressing (see page 133). Leave for an hour before serving, if you can.

* Dress a rinsed and drained can of mixed pulses with vinaigrette dressing (see page 133) and sprinkle with fresh herbs.

* Mix cooked, diced potatoes with a selection of chopped onion or spring onion (scallion), cooked peas, chopped mushrooms or (bell) peppers. Blend a little curry powder or paste into 45 ml/3 tbsp mayonnaise (see page 134) and stir gently into the potato salad.

* Cook small pasta shapes in chicken stock instead of water, then drain well. Mix with chunks of canned tuna and squares of canned pimientos, season well with salt and pepper and dress with a little vinaigrette (see page 133).

* Don't just automatically buy the same type of iceberg or Webb's lettuce, there's loads more choice on the supermarket or greengrocers' shelves. Go for a contrast of flavours and textures; risk an unusual combination. You can choose from: little gem, lambs' lettuce, oakleaf, lollo rosso, lollo biondo, dandelion, spinach leaves, cos (romaine), Chinese leaves (stem lettuce), curly endive (frisée) – the variety is almost endless!

* Mix drained, diced cucumber into Greek yoghurt with a little clear honey and garlic, if liked, and season with salt and freshly ground black pepper. Sprinkle with plenty of chopped fresh mint and serve this tzatziki as a salad or a dip.

* Mix drained canned sweetcorn (corn) with drained chopped pimientos, a chopped tomato and a few chopped mushrooms. Dress with a vinaigrette dressing (see below).

* Toss cubes of feta cheese with sliced onions and tomatoes and dress with olive oil and black pepper.

* Combine walnuts and sliced apples with chopped celery and salad leaves and a light mayonnaise (see page 134).

* Sprinkle salads with chopped nuts, chopped fresh herbs, crumbled cheese, crisply fried pieces of bacon, small croûtons of fried bread or slivers of canned smoked mussels.

Salad Dressings

* **Basic vinaigrette dressing:** blend 15 ml/1 tbsp white wine vinegar, 45 ml/3 tbsp oil, 5 ml/1 tsp mild mustard, salt and freshly ground black pepper.

* Choose from these flavours to add to a basic vinaigrette: 15 ml/1 tbsp chopped fresh herbs; 2 crushed anchovies; 15 ml/1 tbsp chopped capers or gherkins (cornichons).

* **Soy dressing:** blend 60 ml/4 tbsp soy sauce, 15 ml/1 tbsp oil, 15 ml/1 tbsp lemon juice, 5 ml/1 tsp ground ginger and 20 ml/4 tsp clear honey. Use for basting, or blend with 75 ml/5 tbsp water to make a dressing.

* **Mayonnaise** only takes minutes to make. Use a processor or large bowl and whisk. To keep a bowl still while you are whisking and pouring, place it on the work surface next to the edge, wrap a tea towel around the bowl so the two ends hang over the edge and lean against them. Blend 1 egg, 1 egg yolk, 2.5 ml/1 tsp mustard powder, 30 ml/2 tbsp lemon juice, 15 ml/ 1 tbsp white wine vinegar, salt and pepper. Gradually add 375 ml/13 fl oz/1½ cups oil, whisking or blending all the time until the mayonnaise thickens.

* You can blend any number of flavours into mayonnaise to make different dressings or dips. To 250 ml/8 fl oz/1 cup of mayonnaise, try adding: 3 crushed anchovies; 30 ml/2 tbsp finely chopped watercress, spring onions (scallions) or celery leaves; 50 g/2 oz/ 1 small jar caviare (or Danish lumpfish roe); a few crushed garlic cloves; 15 ml/1 tbsp made mustard; 15 ml/1 tbsp curry powder; 25 g/1 oz/ 2 tbsp crumbled blue cheese; 50 g/2 oz/½ cup finely chopped cooked prawns (shrimp) or crab sticks; 45 ml/3 tbsp puréed beetroot (red beet).

* Lighten mayonnaise with a little fromage frais or plain yoghurt, or use these as the base for a salad dressing. Blend in salt and pepper and a little wine or herb vinegar, then sieved hard-boiled (hard-cooked) eggs. If you don't have soured (dairy sour) cream, add a little lemon juice to double (heavy) cream.

* **Thousand island dressing:** blend 15 ml/1 tbsp tomato purée (paste), 15 ml/1 tbsp each finely chopped red and green (bell) pepper and gherkin (cornichon) and 1 chopped hard-boiled (hard-cooked) egg into 150 ml/¼ pt/⅔ cup mayonnaise.

BARBECUE DESSERTS

Desserts are not generally the most important part of a barbecue, but they do round off a meal nicely, especially if you are entertaining. Fruit is an excellent choice, not only because it barbecues well but also because it offers a good taste counterpoint to a rich main course. Ice cream is always a summer favourite, especially with children, so keep some in the freezer and dress it up for the occasion.

Melon and Grapes with Brie

The number of people this delicious dish will serve will, of course, depend on the size of the fruit. You can use any types of melon in any combination.

Serves 6

	METRIC	IMPERIAL	AMERICAN
Cantaloupe melon	1	1	1
Honeydew melon	1	1	1
Watermelon	½	½	½
Seedless (pitless) grapes	225 g	8 oz	½ lb
Fromage frais	90 ml	6 tbsp	6 tbsp
Brie cheese	100 g	4 oz	¼ lb
Flaked (slivered) almonds	50 g	2oz	½ cup

1   Cut the melons into wedges, discarding the seeds and peel, and arrange on serving plates. Arrange the grapes on top.

2   Place a spoonful of fromage frais at the side of each plate.

3   Cut the Brie into wedges and sit the cheese on a piece of foil. Barbecue for about 30 seconds on each side until warm and slightly runny. Place on top of the fruits.

4   Sprinkle with flaked almonds and serve at once.

Preparation time 10 minutes
Cooking time 1 minute

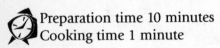

Bananas Foster

Serves 4

	METRIC	IMPERIAL	AMERICAN
Butter or margarine, melted	40 g	1½ oz	3 tbsp
Light brown sugar	45 ml	3 tbsp	3 tbsp
Pinch of ground cinnamon			
Pinch of grated nutmeg			
Bananas, halved lengthways	4	4	4
To serve:			
Vanilla ice cream			
Chopped mixed nuts	60 ml	4 tbsp	4 tbsp

1   Mix the butter with the sugar, cinnamon and nutmeg. Brush the mixture over the bananas. Place on a sheet of foil.

2   Barbecue for about 5 minutes until soft and brown.

3   Transfer to serving dishes and top with ice cream and nuts.

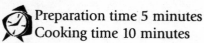 Preparation time 5 minutes
Cooking time 10 minutes

Pears with Coffee Liqueur Cream

An orange liqueur also tastes good in the cream. Add a little orange juice to the flavoured butter to enhance the taste.

Serves 4

	METRIC	IMPERIAL	AMERICAN
Pears	4	4	4
Butter or margarine, melted	40 g	1½ oz	3 tbsp
Light brown sugar	100 g	4 oz	½ cup
For the sauce:			
Fromage frais	225 g	8 oz	1 cup
Whipped cream	250 ml	8 fl oz	1 cup
Plain yoghurt	250 ml	8 fl oz	1 cup
Coffee liqueur	90 ml	6 tbsp	6 tbsp
Pinch of grated nutmeg			

1 Peel and core the pears and slice them thickly or cut them into wedges.

2 Mix the melted butter or margarine and half the sugar and brush over the pears. Arrange on a piece of foil.

3 Barbecue the pears for about 5 minutes until warm.

4 Blend together the fromage frais, cream, remaining sugar, yoghurt, liqueur and nutmeg.

5 Place the pears on serving plates and top with the liqueur cream.

 Preparation time 10 minutes
Cooking time 5 minutes

Orange Chestnut Kebabs

Serves 4

	METRIC	IMPERIAL	AMERICAN
Can of chestnuts, drained	400 g	14 oz	1 large
Butter or margarine, melted	50 g	2 oz	¼ cup
Grated orange rind	10 ml	2 tsp	2 tsp
To serve:			
Light brown sugar	15 ml	1 tbsp	1 tbsp
Double (heavy) or whipping cream, whipped	150 ml	¼ pt	⅔ cup

1 Thread the chestnuts on to soaked wooden skewers.

2 Mix the butter with the orange rind and brush over the chestnuts. Barbecue for about 5 minutes, turning frequently and brushing with flavoured butter.

3 Sprinkle with sugar and serve with whipped cream.

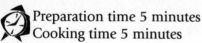 Preparation time 5 minutes
Cooking time 5 minutes

Chocolate Sandwiches

Especially popular with children, who can make up their own parcels while you are preparing the barbecue.

Serves 6

	METRIC	IMPERIAL	AMERICAN
Plain (semi-sweet) chocolate	200 g	7 oz	1 block
Marshmallows	12	12	12
Digestive biscuits (Graham crackers)	12	12	12

1 Break the chocolate into squares.

2 Arrange the chocolate and marshmallows on top of half the biscuits, then top with the other biscuits to make sandwiches. Wrap individually in foil.

3 Place the foil parcels on the barbecue for about 1–3 minutes. Serve at once.

Preparation time 10 minutes
Cooking time 3 minutes

Simple Fruit Ideas

✳ A bowl of fresh fruit is the simplest and can be quite a spectacular barbecue dessert. And there's nothing better than fruit to counter the sometimes rich flavours of the barbecue. Serve with a cheese board too, if liked. There's no need for a vast range of fruits: two or three choices is plenty for an impromptu occasion, so simply arrange what you have attractively in a large bowl or on a platter.

✳ If you are buying specially, choose just three or four fruits which offer a contrast in texture and colour to make a stunning display for your table centre and a delicious end to the meal.

✳ Although we can now buy almost anything at almost any time of the year, choosing fruits in season usually means that you get the best value and the best quality.

✳ Buy one large water melon and cut it into thin crescents – deliciously refreshing if a little messy!

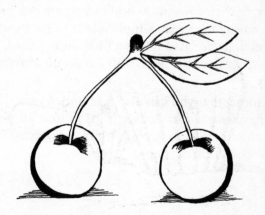

Fruit Salads

* A fruit salad is slightly more sophisticated. Select three or four different fruits with complementary colours and flavours. (Bananas tend to discolour and go very soft so are best saved for hot dishes.) You can use whatever you have available; or try the following combinations: apples, melon, kiwi fruit and raspberries; pineapple, pears and mango; peaches, plums and apricots; oranges, grapes, pineapple and apples; blackberries, apples and redcurrants.

* Remove any cores or stones (pits) from fresh fruits. Whether you peel fruit is up to you. Some pears, for example, have a tasty skin, while others are rather coarse and might spoil the salad. To peel soft-skinned fruit, such as peaches, dip them in boiling water for about 20 seconds, then transfer to cold water and peel off the skin.

* Dice the fruit neatly in equal bite-sized pieces. Always have some lemon juice handy so that you can sprinkle it over apples, peaches or pears as soon as you cut them to prevent them from discolouring. Diced fruits will create their own juice; don't waste any while you are preparing the salad, simply add it to the bowl. If you feel that the salad needs a little more liquid, add a little orange or apple juice with a dash of sherry or brandy.

* Don't forget that you can also add tinned fruits if you don't have enough fresh. Buy fruits in fruit juice or a light syrup for a fresh flavour; fruits in heavy syrup tend to be a little cloying.

* If you do have a sweet tooth and want to add a sugar syrup to the fruit salad, boil 275 g/10 oz/1¼ cups sugar with 600 ml/1 pt/2½ cups water and a squeeze of lemon juice until it is the consistency you prefer. Leave to cool before pouring over the fruit.

* A few fresh or frozen strawberries – sliced if they are large – or raspberries can be scattered over the top for effect. Or, if you have just one kiwi fruit left, arrange it on top of the salad rather than mixing it in with the other fruits.

* Garnish the fruit salad with a few fresh mint leaves and serve it on its own, or with a little cream or crème fraîche. Ice creams and sorbets also make good accompaniments.

Barbecued Fruits

Barbecuing fruits makes a simple and tasty dessert and is a great way of using up the now-perfect hot coals!

* Arrange sliced fruits on a piece of foil, dot with butter and sprinkle lightly with sugar and a touch of ground cinnamon or freshly grated nutmeg. Sprinkle with a little rum or brandy, if you like. Seal the foil tightly, then place on the barbecue for about 15 minutes. Try: thickly sliced peaches, pear halves, orange segments, pineapple rings, banana halves, sliced apples.

* Cinnamon and nutmeg are wonderful spices for sprinkling over fruit before cooking. Nutmeg is at its best if freshly grated as it loses its pungency very quickly.

* Don't ignore herbs with fruit. That old favourite mint goes particularly well with fruits and so does rosemary.

* Alternatively, try kebabs. Use firm fruits such as pineapple, apples, apricots, plums or kiwi fruit in a range of attractive colours. Use just two or three fruits for each kebab, cut them into even-sized chunks and thread alternately on to soaked wooden skewers.

* Whether you are cooking whole fruit or preparing kebabs, soak fruits in a little dessert wine, sherry or your favourite liqueur for 30 minutes before barbecuing. Brush with melted butter or a little oil while they are cooking.

* You can barbecue bananas on the rack or even directly on the coals in their skins; they only take a few minutes to heat through and soften. Take great care when eating, though, as the whole thing gets very hot!

Ice Cream Ideas

* Dress up ordinary ice cream with a sprinkling of chopped nuts, sugar strands, chopped fresh or dried fruits or a drizzle of maple syrup, flower honey, your favourite ice cream sauce or fruit purée.

* Cut two flavours of ice cream – preferably in contrasting colours – into 1 cm/½ in cubes and serve on its own, or with similar-sized cubes of fruit.

* Layer scoops of ice cream, whipped cream, chopped nuts, fresh cake crumbs, soft fruits, fruit purée or sauce in a sundae glass and top with a swirl of cream.

* Melt a chopped Mars bar or two with a little milk gently in the microwave or in a bowl over a pan of simmering water to pour over your ice cream.

* Plain sweet biscuits make tasty accompaniments.

Other Dessert Ideas

* Sorbets and mousses make good barbecue desserts and can be bought or made in advance and kept in the fridge or freezer. Dress them up with some grated chocolate, grated orange rind, chopped nuts, fruit purée or fruit slices, depending on the flavour.

* Poach a few ready-to-eat dried apricot halves in apple juice with a slug of white wine or sherry for 10 minutes, then leave them to soak for as long as possible. Drain and serve topped with a spoonful of cranberry sauce and a swirl of cream.

* Cold desserts are most welcome. Keep a frozen gâteau or special dessert such as a lemon tart in the freezer; it will only take a couple of hours to defrost.

* Mix together equal quantities of strong black coffee with brandy or rum and spoon over sponge fingers or slices of sponge cake in a bowl until they are soaked. Top with lightly whisked Mascarpone cheese and sprinkle with grated chocolate.

* Pancakes with honey, sugar or maple syrup and lemon juice make a popular dessert. Make them in advance, interleaf with greaseproof (waxed) paper and reheat in the oven while you are eating.

* Buy brandy snap baskets or chocolate cups and fill with fruit and/or ice cream.

* Cut filo pastry into 13 cm/5 in squares, brush with melted butter and place two or three squares on top of each other. Place a spoonful of mincemeat or some very thinly sliced dessert apples and a little ground cinnamon in the centre and scrunch together to form little purses. Brush with more melted butter. Bake in a preheated oven at 200°C/400°F/gas mark 6 for about 10 minutes until crisp. Serve with cream.

* Dissolve 100 g/4 oz/½ cup caster (superfine) sugar over a very gentle heat until golden brown. Remove from the heat and add 60 ml/4 tbsp lemon juice and 750 ml/1¼ pts/3 cups water. Return to the heat, bring to the boil, then simmer for 3 minutes. Leave to cool, then stir in four sliced oranges and chill for as long as possible, preferably 4 hours.

* As a last-minute dessert, sandwich shortcake triangles together with whipped cream and soft fruit. Top with a swirl of cream and a little grated chocolate.

* Swirl a spoonful of colourful fruit purée, sieved jam (conserve) or bottled chocolate sauce into thick plain yoghurt for a simple but dramatic dessert.

* Purée a tub of ricotta cheese with about half the quantity of drained canned peaches, then pile on slices of crusty bread or toast and sprinkle with soft brown sugar.

REFRESHING DRINKS

In hot weather, everyone will need plenty to drink.
Offer a range of drinks such as light wines, beer and
lager, and plenty of soft drinks, but don't go overboard
on choice. Large jugs of iced water are also very
welcome. Here are a few more interesting ideas for you
to try.

~~~~~~~~~~~~

Mango Cooler

*If you don't have lime juice, use slightly less lemon juice,
adding just enough to sharpen the flavour. Float some lime or
lemon slices on the top if you have some.*

Serves 4

	METRIC	IMPERIAL	AMERICAN
Can of mango in juice	400 g	14 oz	1 large
Dry white wine	300 ml	½ pt	1¼ cups
Fizzy mineral water	250 ml	8 fl oz	1 cup
Lime juice	30 ml	2 tbsp	2 tbsp
Ice cubes			

1 Purée the mango with its juice.

2 Mix with the remaining ingredients in a large jug.

 Preparation time 5 minutes

Strawberry Fruit Punch

Substitute any summer fruits for the strawberries, or use canned fruit.

Serves 6

	METRIC	IMPERIAL	AMERICAN
Strawberries	450 g	1 lb	1 lb
Caster (superfine) sugar	75 g	3 oz	1/3 cup
Brandy	175 ml	6 fl oz	3/4 cup
Bottle of dry white wine, chilled	1	1	1
Soda water or mineral water			

1 Slice the strawberries, sprinkle with sugar and pour over the brandy. Leave to stand for as long as possible.

2 Add the white wine and soda or mineral water to taste.

Preparation time 10 minutes
Marinating time as long as possible

Red Wine Punch

The fruit is for effect as well as flavour; use whatever you have to hand. Use less lemonade for a more heady mixture.

Serves 6

	METRIC	IMPERIAL	AMERICAN
Bottle of red wine	1	1	1
Brandy	60 ml	4 tbsp	4 tbsp
Port	60 ml	4 tbsp	4 tbsp
Lemonade	600 ml	1 pt	2½ cups
Lemon, sliced	1	1	1
Apple, sliced	1	1	1
Orange, sliced	1	1	1
Ice cubes			

Mix together all the ingredients in a large bowl or jug and float with ice cubes to serve.

 Preparation time 5 minutes

Golden Tea Punch

Sweeten the drink to taste with honey or a little sugar.

Serves 6

	METRIC	IMPERIAL	AMERICAN
Ginger ale	450 ml	¾ pt	2 cups
Pineapple juice	300 ml	½ pt	1¼ cups
Orange juice	250 ml	8 fl oz	1 cup
Cold strong black tea	250 ml	8 fl oz	1 cup
Lime juice	90 ml	6 tbsp	6 tbsp
Clear honey	15 ml	1 tbsp	1 tbsp
Ice cubes			

Mix together all the ingredients and serve at once.

 Preparation time 5 minutes

Banana Whip

Serves 2-4

	METRIC	IMPERIAL	AMERICAN
Milk	450 ml	¾ pt	2 cups
Ripe bananas, chopped	1-2	1-2	1-2
Scoops of vanilla ice cream	2	2	2

1 Blend the milk, banana and ice cream until frothy.

2 Pour into a jug or glasses and add ice cubes.

 Preparation time 5 minutes

Hawaiian Iced Coffee

Serves 2-4

	METRIC	IMPERIAL	AMERICAN
Can of pineapple in juice	300 g	11 oz	1 large
Milk	300 ml	½ pt	1¼ cups
Instant coffee	15 ml	1 tbsp	1 tbsp
Hot water	10 ml	2 tsp	2 tsp
Scoops of vanilla ice cream	2	2	2
Demerara sugar	10 ml	2 tsp	2 tsp
Freshly ground nutmeg			

1 Blend the pineapple pieces and juice, then add the milk and process again.

2 Dissolve the coffee in the hot water and add to the blender. Blend until well mixed. Taste and add a little more dissolved coffee if you like.

3 Add the ice cream and process briefly.

4 Pour into a jug or individual glasses and sprinkle with sugar and a little nutmeg.

 Preparation time 10 minutes

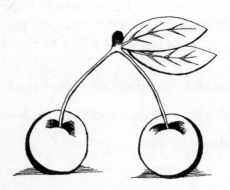

More Drink Ideas

✳ For a hot outdoor meal, always make sure you have plenty of drinks and plenty of ice cubes.

✳ Keep the options simple: red or chilled white wine; lager or beer; soft drinks.

✳ Special occasion? For all but the *cognoscenti*, well chilled Bucks Fizz is just as welcome made with a good sparkling wine. Mix two parts 'bubbly' with one part fresh orange juice.

✳ Dilute lemon squash with soda water, sweeten with a little honey and float thinly sliced lemons and ice cubes in the jug.

✳ Fruit juices can be heavy to serve with food. Try a mixture of orange and pineapple juice topped up with an equal quantity of soda water or mineral water.

✳ Elderflower cordial diluted with sparkling mineral water and lots of ice is very cool and refreshing.

✳ Make a jug of iced tea. Add a few mint sprigs and a sliced lemon to weak tea, sweeten to taste and chill for at least 30 minutes.

✳ Make milky coffee and chill it thoroughly. Whisk in a few scoops of vanilla ice cream before serving with ice cubes.

✳ Herbal teas or fruit teas can be more refreshing than coffee when served after a meal on a hot day. Alternatively, offer China tea served with a slice of lemon.

BARBECUE PARTY CHECKLIST

So the weather's fine and you've decided to invite the neighbours round to celebrate the fact that the sun is shining. What do you need? Have you forgotten anything? Do you need to buy anything extra? Use this handy checklist to eliminate the stress and make sure everything goes smoothly. You can photocopy these pages and use them to jot down your menu and any extras which make your barbecue a real inspiration!

How Many Guests?

- [ ] Adults
- [ ] Children

What Do I Need?

- [ ] Barbecue and equipment
- [ ] Charcoal
- [ ] Firelighters
- [ ] Matches

- [ ] Tables
- [ ] Tablecloth and napkins
- [ ] Chairs
- [ ] Lights
- [ ] Music

☐ Crockery
☐ Cutlery
☐ Glasses
☐ Serving dishes
☐ Serving cutlery

Food
Starters/nibbles

Meat dishes

Chicken dishes

Vegetable dishes

Side dishes

Desserts

Drinks
Special recipes

☐ Red wine
☐ White wine
☐ Beer
☐ Lager
☐ Soft drinks

Last-minute Barbecue Plan

* Invite guests and work out numbers. Remember to tell them what time to arrive and what time you aim to serve the food.

* Check barbecue and equipment. List anything extra you need (do you have enough charcoal?)

* Prepare the menu. Mark any oven-cooked dishes that need longer cooking time.

* Prepare the drinks list.

* Check food stocks and send out/go to the shops to buy any equipment, foods or drinks that you need.

* Prepare foods for marinating and set to marinate.

* Prepare foods for barbecuing, cover and store in the fridge.

* Prepare side salads and side dishes, cover and store in the fridge.

* Set the tables.

* Set out the drinks.

* Set up the fire.

* Light the fire at least 30 minutes before you want to start cooking. Preheat the oven, if necessary.

* Put any additional dishes in the oven.

* Allow time to stop for a cup of tea (or something stronger), a shower and change.

* Lay out the foods ready to be cooked; cover them carefully.

* Be ready when your guests arrive.

* Have a great barbecue!

INDEX